ORANGES

Edible

Series Editor: Andrew F. Smith

EDIBLE is a revolutionary new series of books dedicated to food and drink that explores the rich history of cuisine. Each book reveals the global history and culture of one type of food or beverage.

Already published

Apple Erika Janik *Beef* Lorna Piatti-Farnell *Bread* William Rubel *Cake* Nicola Humble *Caviar* Nichola Fletcher *Champagne* Becky Sue Epstein *Cheese* Andrew Dalby *Chocolate* Sarah Moss and Alexander Badenoch *Cocktails* Joseph M. Carlin *Curry* Colleen Taylor Sen *Dates* Nawal Nasrallah *Gin* Lesley Jacobs Solmonson *Hamburger* Andrew F. Smith *Herbs* Gary Allen *Hot Dog* Bruce Kraig *Ice Cream* Laura B. Weiss *Lemon* Toby Sonneman *Lobster* Elisabeth Townsend *Milk* Hannah Velten *Offal* Nina Edwards *Olive* Fabrizia Lanza *Oranges* Clarissa Hyman *Pancake* Ken Albala *Pie* Janet Clarkson *Pizza* Carol Helstosky *Pork* Katharine M. Rogers *Potato* Andrew F. Smith *Rum* Richard Foss *Sandwich* Bee Wilson *Soup* Janet Clarkson *Spices* Fred Czarra *Tea* Helen Saberi *Whiskey* Kevin R. Kosar *Wine* Marc Millon

Oranges

A Global History

Clarissa Hyman

REAKTION BOOKS

For Phil Gusack

Published by Reaktion Books Ltd
33 Great Sutton Street
London EC1V 0DX, UK
www.reaktionbooks.co.uk

First published 2013

Printed and bound in China by C&C Offset Printing Co., Ltd

British Library Cataloguing in Publication Data

Hyman, Clarissa.
Oranges : a global history. – (Edible)
1. Oranges. 2. Oranges–History. 3. Orange growers.
I. Title II. Series
641.3´431-DC23

ISBN 978 1 78023 099 3

Contents

I

The History of Oranges

In a word, these trees charm the eye, satisfy the smell, gratify
the taste, serving both luxury and art, and presenting to
astonished man a union of all delights.
Giorgio Gallesio, *Orange Culture: A Treatise on the
Citrus Family* (1811)

Oranges may not be the only fruit, but they are one of
the most romantic. For centuries, they have captured the
imagination, beguiled with fiery golden hues and intoxicating fragrance, and sensuously refreshed our palates, yet
their precise history remains as elusive and tantalizing as
their scent.

One key theory by the botanist Walter T. Swingle held
that the proto-parents of the citrus family originated in the
New Guinea-Melanesia region before the continents of Asia
and Australia broke apart,

> but its evolution into many different species took place
> chiefly on the mainland of southeastern Asia. In fact, it
> is only there that the most highly developed species of
> Citrus can be considered as indigenous.[1]

More recently, botanists David Mabberley and Andrew Beattie have supported this view of the dispersal of the earliest true species of citrus as 'floating fruit' on westward-flowing equatorial currents millions of years ago.[2] The focus thus became 'Monsoonia', the mountainous parts of southern China and northeast India where most commercial species and cultivars originated.[3] The Japanese botanist T. Tanaka (1885–1976) narrowed this to northern Burma and Assam, while the eminent scientist and sinophile Joseph Needham (1900–1995) wrote:

> There can be no manner of doubt that the original home and habitat of these trees was on the eastern and southern slopes of the Himalayan massif; a fact which is reflected in the presence of the maximum number of old-established varieties in the Chinese culture-area, as also in the extreme antiquity of the Chinese literary references.[4]

Later studies point to Yunnan, along with nearby areas of India, Burma and southern China, as the primitive centres of origin.[5]

With such profusion of growth and botanical development, it was inevitable that seeds and trees would spread – by bird, animal or man, sea or land. Routes were various, but whether it was to be by way of southern India, Arabia and the Nile or through Asia Minor, citrus was set to circle the world.

The earliest mention of oranges and their 'congeners' is in the *Yu Kung* chapter on geo-botany in the *Shu Ching* (Book of Historical Documents), which Needham says may date back to the eighth or ninth century BC. Han Fei, a philosopher from the second century BC, describes a much earlier discourse that contrasts the characteristics of oranges and thorny lime bushes (sour trifoliate). It becomes a parable of the

Chinese porcelain vase painted in underglaze blue and overglazed enamels on gilt, 1760–80. In one decorative panel a lady in a garden is being offered a citrus fruit by a richly dressed young man.

care women need to take when choosing young men. Another mention, in 600 BC, discusses the etiquette of peeling an orange at a princely court. *Chü Lu* (The Orange Record), written in AD 1178 by Han Yen-Chih, is the oldest known monograph on the orange and describes 28 varieties of sweet, sour and mandarin oranges, including one which 'tastes sweet like milk'.[6]

So, like Suzanne in the Leonard Cohen song, we feed on tea and oranges that came all the way from China, although the first fruit were often dry, thick-skinned and seedy. The Chinese, however, readily became expert growers, their horticultural skills sharpened by both cultural isolation and favourable natural conditions. Increased demand plus better communication between the provinces soon led to the large-scale planting of commercial orchards. According to Needham, 'It is safe to conclude that citrus fruits were being grown industrially for market . . . for at least half a century before people in Europe encountered the first of the group to become known to them.'[7]

Oranges were generally less valued for nourishment than for aesthetic, medical or olfactory qualities, but they were also preserved in honey or used to season vegetables, tea and wine. Su Tung-p'o (AD 1031) lyrically describes the gathering of sweet oranges to make a wine that is 'worthy of turquoize [*sic*] ladles, silver flagons, purple gauze, and green silk wrappers'.[8] His description of 'a thousand yellow-headed slaves' in the groves of the wealthy still strikes a compelling note.

In India, a medical treatise *c.* AD 100 was the first to mention the fruit by a term we recognize today. *Naranga* or *narangi* derives from the Sanskrit, originally meaning 'per-fume within', but thereafter the word trail is long and winding.

Citrons were the first citrus fruit commonly known to the classical world, but to what extent the Romans were also famil-iar with oranges remains disputed. Samuel Tolkowsky argues that they were grown, albeit for purely ornamental purposes. As evidence, he points to a Pompeii mosaic that features 'an orange affected with a type of excrescence with which every orange-grower is familiar', and garlands of oranges on the fourth-century mosaics in S. Constanza, Rome.[9] Alfred C. Andrews generally took the Tolkowsky line, albeit with reser-vations, when he wrote,

> It is also reasonable to assume that orange culture was introduced into Lower Egypt about the beginning of the Christian era, that shipments of the fruit were made

from this area to central Italy, and that attempts were made to raise orange trees there.[10]

On the other hand, L. Ramón-Laca notes that it is striking that there are no mentions of different citrus fruit until the time of the Arabic authors: 'This fact points directly to the responsibility of the Muslims, except in the case of the citron, for the main diffusion of the different citrus and its subsequent introduction to the Mediterranean basin.'[11]

After the Lombard invasion in AD 568, the luxurious gardens of the Romans were largely wiped out. Citrus disappeared, except in some southern areas of the Mediterranean world, until the Arabs revived the art of citriculture a few hundred years later, bringing the bitter 'Seville' orange from Arabia to North Africa and Spain along with Persian techniques of cultivation, planting and irrigation. A story Tolkowsky tells illustrates the profound love citrus held for the conquerors: in Baghdad, a Caliph had a grove whose 'interlaced branches were loaded with red and yellow fruit glittering like stars'. When deprived of his throne and blinded by his nephew, to prevent the latter from enjoying the beautiful orchard, he pretended to have buried treasure there. The nephew promptly dug up all the trees.

Citrus held a special place in the Islamic soul, being loved for its graceful form, the intensity of its evergreen leaves and its hedonistic blossom. The flowers, fruit and leaves were also used in medicine, gastronomy and the cosmetic arts. The wood was fashioned into the most beautiful furniture; even the twig ends were shredded and used as disposable toothbrushes.[12]

In turn, the Crusades created an interest in northern Europe in exotic new produce brought back by the returning warriors in the twelfth and thirteenth centuries. These included a

Babur, the first Mughal emperor, supervising the laying out of the Garden of Fidelity outside Kabul, *c.* 1590, opaque watercolour and gold on paper.

variety of sour orange called *bigardia*, and the bittersweet fruits must have seemed irresistible tokens of azure skies and soft sunshine. Queen Eleanor of Castile, who would have grown up knowing about citrus fruit, arrived in Acre in Israel in 1271 for a two-year stay with her husband Edward 1. Years later, she perhaps had a Proustian moment, buying fifteen lemons and seven oranges from a Spanish ship in Portsmouth.

According to Barbara Santich, citrus had become reasonably common in Italy by the thirteenth century, although a century later it was still novel enough in Prato for Francesco Datini to have a large orange tree as a status symbol.[13] In Provence, Catherine de Medici gave her guests gifts of citrons and oranges. By the end of the sixteenth century, Santich notes, Swiss visitors to Perpignan and Barcelona marvelled at the numbers of citrus trees in the streets, and were amazed in Montpellier at the cheapness of oranges which people threw at each other during Mardi Gras.[14]

How the sweet Chinese orange arrived in Europe is uncertain. The popular story is that João de Castro was the first to bring a tree to Lisbon in the mid-sixteenth century, and from this all others were cultivated. However, the first written reference dates back to 1472 – a bill of sale from a trader in Savona, now in Liguria, Italy, that mentions 15,000 sweet oranges. In the account of Vasco da Gama's voyage in 1498 by Alvaro Velho, 'fine' orange trees are mentioned that are 'better than those of Portugal',[15] but whether this means sweet oranges were known earlier in Europe or not, is unclear.

Tolkowsky believed that they were, and argued that the Talmudic expression 'sweet citrons' refers to sweet oranges. He also quoted Platina who, in 1475 after a decade of work on his manuscript, stated that sweet oranges are 'almost always suitable for the stomach as a first course and the tart ones may be sweetened with sugar'. As further proof, he

Johann Walther, *Branch of Orange Tree in Bloom, Oranges and Shells*, 1661, gouache on vellum.

Postage stamp, Turkey. The name of the fruit on the stamp – *portakal* – reflects the Portuguese role in the journey of the orange.

KIBRIS TÜRK FEDERE DEVLETİ POSTALARI

60 M.

PORTAKAL – CITRUS SINENSIS

noted that Louis XI gave sweet oranges from Provence to St Francis in 1483 as a gift 'for the holy man who eats neither fish nor meat'.[16]

Horticulturalist Herbert John Webber, too, came down on the side of an existing familiarity, suggesting that the sweet orange reached Europe sometime in the early part of the fifteenth century, probably through the commercial Genoese trade routes from Arabia, Palestine and India.

> If the sweet orange were at that time unknown to da Gama, it would seem astonishing that he failed to describe it as different from the known sorts. None of the travelers of this epoch showed surprise at sight of this fruit, as they did on seeing many others, from which it may be deduced that they were already familiar with the sweet orange and it was no longer a novelty.[17]

The sixteenth-century Italian poet Andrea Navagero described splendid sweet orange trees in the kitchen garden of the king at Seville; and Webber noted that the historian-monk Leandro Alberti referred to the sweet fruit of the immense plantations of cultivated trees he saw in Sicily,

Calabria, Liguria and elsewhere in Italy in 1550: 'It is clearly impossible that this extensive culture of the sweet orange in Liguria at the beginning of the sixteenth century could have come from the Portuguese importation, since that did not take place earlier than the beginning of that century' (perhaps about 1520).[18]

Whether these early 'sweet' oranges were actually sweet or bittersweet will probably remain unclarified. The fact that citrus fruit is generally known in Italy as *agrumi* (meaning sour or tart fruit) points to the latter. However, Tolkowsky contends that there was little distinction between sweet and sour oranges in the fourteenth and fifteenth centuries because they were used as a condiment or medicinal agent, not as an eating fruit. So it is perhaps possible that the Portuguese, post-Vasco da Gama, only introduced a new – and better-tasting – variety of sweet orange, not a new species. Nonetheless, it became known as the 'Portingall' or Portugal orange, a term still echoed

In this British bowl from *c.* 1734, a symbolic orange tree unites William IV and Princess Anne of Hanover.

James Gillray, *The Orangerie or the Dutch Cupid Reposing after the Fatigues of Planting*, 1796. In this hand-coloured etching William V, Prince of Orange, is depicted as a fat, naked Cupid reclining on a platform of grass and flowers. He is leaning on a bag of money marked '24,000,000 ducats'. In the foreground are a number of orange trees, with each orange bearing a likeness of the prince.

in the Greek word *portokalo* and the Turkish *portakal*, then increasingly as the China orange.

The impact was immense. The Chinese had taken citri-culture to new heights, as witnessed by the Jesuit missionary Alvaro Semedo in 1640: 'The oranges of Canton might well be queens over our own, in fact some people hold that they are not so much oranges as muscat grapes disguised.'[19]

But what of the link between the fruit and the French town of the same name? Tolkowsky is categorical: 'There is no other connection than that which exists between any two homonyms, namely a purely accidental similarity of sound.'[20] The town became the possession of the German William of Nassau, Prince of Orange, who founded the Dutch Republic and the House of Orange and adopted the colour. In turn,

Inevitably the fruit as well as the colour became a symbol of the House of Orange-Nassau, as evidenced by this sculpture in the market square of the German town of Oranienbaum.

this led to the naming of the Orange River in South Africa; Cape Orange in Brazil; the Orangemen of Northern Ireland; Orange, New Jersey; Orangeville; and more.

The connection between the fruit and the colour also has its own story. An early Italian word for orange was *melarancio* (fruit of the orange tree). From this came the Old French *orenge*, adopted in turn by Middle English. According to the Oxford English Dictionary, the words 'orenge' and 'orange' were first recorded in the fifteenth century; the colour orange was usually referred to as 'yellow-red' or 'tawny' until the sixteenth century, which saw the introduction of New World pumpkins and Dutch 'orange' carrots. Mark Morton suggests that a word for the colour was not necessary before then, because 'there weren't many things in dreary medieval England that actually needed to be described as orange'.[21]

On his second voyage in 1493, Columbus brought citrus seeds to Haiti and the Caribbean. Robert Willard Hodgson considers it likely that the Spanish took the bittersweet orange to both Florida and South America, 'for it was early found in the former and occurs extensively in Paraguay where it comprises an important source of oil of petit grain'.[22] Whatever the species, the trees spread rapidly throughout the islands and in Central and South America. One early visitor reported that the oranges and lemons of Brazil were sweet and huge, the size of two fists put together. The English poet Andrew Marvell (1621–1678) vividly described the trees in 'Bermudas' as 'feral' where 'He hangs in shades the orange bright, / Like golden lamps in a green night'. Soon, oranges and limes were even being shipped back to Europe.

According to John F. Mariani, Hernando de Soto brought the orange to St Augustine, Florida in 1539.[23] With the exception of a grower named Jesse Fish, who shipped an amazing 65,000 oranges to England in 1776, commercial plantings were insignificant until 1821, when the U.S. acquired Florida. By 1871, oranges were ubiquitous: a Dr Baldwin wrote,

> You may eat oranges from morning to night at every plantation along the shore [of the St Johns] while the wild trees, bending with their golden fruit over the water, present an enchanting appearance.[24]

The orange reached California with the founding of the San Diego Mission in 1769, but the first grove of any considerable size was planted at the San Gabriel Mission in 1804. Citrus fruit soon became a key factor in promoting a lifestyle image of sunshine and easy living to attract settlers to the state.

Far away in the Dutch colony of Cape Town, oranges and other fruit and vegetables were introduced from St Helena by the colony's first governor in 1654, and in 1787 oranges were taken to New South Wales with the colonists of the First Fleet.

Back in the Old World, Portuguese ports swarmed with English traders; oranges were shipped in their tens of thousands.[25] In 1562, Lord Burleigh owned a rare, single orange tree; the same year, Sir Francis Carew brought a few from France which he trained against a wall and sheltered with boards and stoves in winter. Sir Walter Raleigh planted orange

Orange grove, St Johns River, Florida, 1887. Once oranges were introduced into Florida, the Spanish traded them with Native Americans. This led to the spread of the naturalized trees along the river and inland. Some of these feral oranges were later domesticated by American homesteaders who, in turn, planted further groves.

Figure of an orange seller from Niderviller, France, *c.* 1770–84. The association of oranges with buxom wenches was readily embraced by artists throughout Europe.

seeds in Surrey; the trees began bearing regular crops in 1595, but were killed by cold in 1739.

John Houghton noted that in seventeenth-century London oranges were 'carried in the eye of all about the streets, we see they are very much consumed by the ordinary people'.[26] Transportation difficulties and rotting, however, prevented their wider availability. Like many other products past their best, they were sold cheaply in the capital either from 'moveable shops that run upon wheels, attended by ill-looking Fellows' or by flirtatious orange-girls in London's theatres, epitomized by the pretty, witty Nell Gwyn, the mistress of Charles II. As Thomas D'Urfey acidly pointed out in the prologue to his play *The Comical History of Don Quixote* (1694), 'The orange-miss that here cajoled the Duke, / May sell her rotten ware without rebuke.'

Samuel Pepys recounted in his diary in 1665 how Mrs Jennings, a maid of honour, dressed as an orange wench to the amusement of all until exposed by her expensive shoes – although we don't know if she also imitated the usual foul-mouthed swearing.

It became increasingly fashionable for the well-to-do of Europe to grow the orange tree even though its hardiness was doubtful, hence Pepys's comment on the 'brave' orange and lemon trees in Lord Wotton's garden two years later. Buying costly imports or, better still, having the time, skill and space to grow your own was an expensive and competitive game of one-upmanship. It would result in some of the most extraordinary pieces of garden architecture ever built. Especially if you were the king of France.

2

Cultivation

Seville may be said to be still . . . the rendezvous of the most
picturesque blackguards in the south of Spain . . . [who]
know of heaven what they see of it through the golden juice
of an orange, as they lie on their backs in the cool shade,
a picture of contentment and sweet idleness.

John Lomas, ed., *O'Shea's Guide to Spain and
Portugal* (London, 1905)

Oranges, like jewels, need a setting. Nature provided the back-
cloth of glossy, jade leaves; it was left to man to construct
the *mise-en-scène*.

Citrus cultivation both challenges and inspires. Garden
design fused with horticultural function is a form of architectural art that can be seen at its most elemental on Pantelleria,
off Sicily. The island has hot, dry summers with little rainfall;
strong winds prevent the trees from growing tall. The centuries-
old solution was to build striking lava-stone enclosures that act
as windshields, absorb night-time moisture, permit aeration
and support the soil.

The Arabs brought new crops, irrigation and landscap-
ing techniques to Al-Andalus, their state in parts of today's
Spain, Portugal and France: groves of citrus marked their

Cathedral Mosque main entrance, as seen from the Los Naranjos patio in Cordoba, Spain.

advancing path for several centuries.[1] Islamic gardens were made for rest and contemplation. Shade and water were the key elements that provided refuge from the hostile world outside their walls. These geometric gardens – a form of paradise on earth – have both sensuality and intellectual precision.

The great fourteenth-century Arab traveller Ibn Battuta described the courtyard of the principal mosque of Malaga as having an 'unequalled beauty [with] exceptionally tall orange trees';[2] in Granada, there are still oranges and lemons in the hanging gardens of the Generalife, the summer palace of the Nasrid emirs. Citrus was everywhere. One can only daydream on reading the words of Lorenzo Valla, an Italian humanist, on a visit to Valencia in the fifteenth century, 'The most remarkable thing, there are gardens not only composed entirely of citrus trees, but with walls of citrus, so that you ask yourself whether these are gardens or rooms.'[3]

This enchanting indoor-outdoor image is mirrored in the words of poet and playwright Félix Arturo Lope de Vega (1562–1635). Writing about the Duke of Alba's beautiful garden at Abadía, he describes how the fruit grows in both winter and summer,

> And the more the mountain is white with snow,
> The more it prides itself upon its everlasting treasure . . .
> On the farther side, along the shining river,
> There are lanes clothed with orange trees
> And portals ingeniously wrought of them.[4]

Tuscany, however, was the cradle of the new Renaissance garden; in Florence, the fashion for collecting citrus trees became all the rage among patricians and wealthy merchants. Botticelli's *Primavera* (1482), for example, depicts Giuliano de' Medici (or possibly Lorenzo di Pierfrancesco de' Medici) posing somewhat self-consciously in an orange grove, the very model of gilded youth.

The Medici created one of the greatest European citrus gardens in 1544 at the Villa di Castello near Florence. The orbs on their escutcheon have variously been interpreted as pawnbrokers' balls, apothecaries' pills or, some say, oranges. The garden was intended to reflect the power and status of the family: a lunette painting of 1600 shows the imposing house flanked by regimented rows of trees. The villa still boasts hundreds of potted citrus varieties, few of which are now grown commercially, including the rare – and brilliantly named – *bizzarria* of Florence.

The plants would have struggled without indoor winter quarters which ensured citrus could survive in the Little Ice Age even as far north as the Italian Lakes. The tradition is still to put out the pots when the mulberries come into leaf. The first structures were fairly basic with the trees protected by straw or wattle fences, but in due course heating, insulation and ventilation improved. To remove and set up again enclosures and roofs, however, was very expensive, so the art of raising trees in boxes developed further.

At the beginning of the sixteenth century, Giovanni Pontano published *De hortis Hesperidum*, which advised planting fruit in wheel-mounted boxes that could be moved to shelter or positioned around banquet tables as a pick-your-own-dessert. In 1628, the English botanist John Parkinson suggested,

> For that purpose, some keepe them in great square boxes, and lift them to and fro by iron hooks on the sides, or cause them to be rowled by trundels, or small wheeles under them, to place them in a house or close gallery.[5]

Detail of Mercury holding a wand to an orange tree, from Sandro Botticelli, *La Primavera*, 1482, tempera on wood. The painting shows Venus in the centre of an orange grove that represents love and fertility.

Horticulturalists around Northern Europe went to great lengths to protect their fragile trees. In the prosperous town of Nuremberg, the silk merchant Johann Christoph Volckamer (1644–1720) commissioned the three-volume *Nuremberg Hesperides* with etchings based on the citrus fruit he himself raised or had sent from Italy. He also described the old wooden, winter *Pomeranzen* houses (*Pomeranze* is the German word for sour orange) with roofs insulated with straw and loam.

This impulse to grow citrus in unsuitable climates had a curious parallel several centuries later during the Communist rule of Hungary in the 1950s. The authorities wanted a domestic crop to replace expensive imported fruit, so trees were planted in deep trenches on the south-facing slopes of Lake Balaton with the notion of covering them completely in winter. Alas, the project was spectacularly unsuccessful, but it did inspire the name of a satirical political magazine, *Magyar Narancs* (Hungarian Oranges).

In the seventeenth century new developments in Dutch technology enabled the production of expanses of clear glass. This changed the architectural scene dramatically, and the buildings became increasingly ornate to reflect the exotic plants they housed. Citrus trees were proof of wealth, and the orangery a major status symbol in the homes of the European

Jan van der Goyen (1596–1656), *Oranje-stoove*, engraving. In the 17th century, systems of heating orangeries and cossseting the trees became ever more elaborate, and an object of interest for aspirational householders.

The Orangery, Potsdam, Berlin, c. 1890–1900.

rich and fashionable. Up to the nineteenth century their design grew ever more ostentatious, flaunting fabulous fountains, grottos and other fantastical features.

Oranges were a favourite decorative motif in interior design: they proliferated across indoor garden scenes, friezes, frescoes, bas relief and metal doors. The glazed terracotta sculptures of the della Robbia family in Florence characteristically used oranges and lemons as well as apples, nuts, foliage and flowers.

After the French king Charles viii returned in 1495 from his disastrous wars in Italy with an enthusiasm for the palaces and gardens of that country, he employed a Neapolitan garden designer to build a large orangery at the chateau of Amboise. Soon after, François i commissioned one for Blois. The competition to build the biggest and the best had begun.

It all came down to money. Olivier de Serres (1539–1619), in a classic seventeenth-century treatise on French agriculture, pointedly wrote,

Oranges, citrons, lemons and other suchlike valuable fruit trees flourish in any climate, provided one is ready to incur the necessary expenditure . . . It is in truth a sport for princes and noblemen to grow these excellent trees in a climate that is contrary to their nature: a luxury, therefore, that is more easily admired than copied.[6]

Few, however, could ever aspire to equal the *ne plus ultra* of orangeries, that of Versailles. Built by Jules Hardouin-Mansart for Louis xiv on plans submitted by André Le Nôtre, it was conceived on an epic, money-no-object scale to project an image of absolute monarchy; like the rest of the gardens, it showcased the skills of the seventeenth-century's greatest artists and scientists. The king had a passion for citrus and his gardeners developed techniques to obtain blossom year-round. Waverley Root observed that the 1,200 orange trees in silver tubs were for show rather than food since Louis, away

The orangery at Versailles, 1850s–70s, photographed by Francis Frith.

Jean-Baptiste Hilaire, *Orange-picking*, 1794, pen and black ink, gouache and watercolour. This picture depicts the Jardin du Roi, a Paris garden created by Louis XIII's doctor and opened to the public in 1636.

at the wars, wrote to his minister, 'Let me know what effect the orange trees at Versailles are making.'[7] Pyramids of oranges, apples and pears were *à la mode* as table decor.

The Versailles orangery took nearly ten years to build but became the talk and envy of the aristocratic world, the venue for garden parties and masked balls. Court historian André Félibien described the heady setting in 1668:

> Their majesties would stroll through these highly scented, bosky thickets. Like a labyrinth, there were many pathways – one lined with 'Portuguese' oranges, another with bitter orange and cherry trees. Others were bordered by apricots and peaches, Dutch redcurrants and different sorts of pear trees.[8]

Legend has it that one of the trees at Versailles dated back nearly 200 years to a cutting originally sent by the queen of Navarre to Queen Anne of Bretagne. It was known as the *Grand Bourbon* and continued to blossom and bear fruit until its death in 1894. In winter, the orangery still houses more than 1,000 trees in traditional Versailles planters with hinged sides; from May to October, they are put outdoors in the *Parterre Bas*.

The orangery at the Schönbrunn in Vienna rivals Versailles in size. Built in 1745, it was more than a Baroque winter home for potted plants: the trees were illuminated as a setting for spectacular royal parties and imperial festivities. The German town of Oranienbaum (where a bronze orange tree in the marketplace symbolizes the House of Orange) also boasts one of the longest orangeries in Europe.

In 1709, the Saxon Elector August the Strong had plans for a voluptuous new dream palace in Dresden. He began with the lavish, decadent orangery, named *Zwinger* because of its location. It included a theatre, waterfall, *Nymphenbad* (a fountain surrounded by statues of nymphs), swimming pool and banqueting space to give guests the impression that they were dining and dancing in the middle of an orange grove. The trees were housed in ornate blue-and-white Ming pots. However, August ran out of funds and after his death in 1733 plans were scaled down and the complex was only completed around a century later.

It was a bitter end – and all for the love of an orange.

3
Classification

The orange tree rivals all for beauty; no other quite has its captivating combination of glamorous green leaves, glowing fruit and wax-white star-shaped flowers with extravagant scent. They can live for up to a century and produce hundreds of fruits, but orange trees are sub tropical plants requiring warmth to survive, no frost and large amounts of water. Depending on the variety, the fruits can remain for some time on the tree once mature, but will not ripen any further after picking.

Citrus belongs to the rue family (*Rutaceae*) and, botanically, the fruit is a berry called a *hesperidium*, but the problem is trying to determine exactly what is being defined. It is the most confusing of fruit. Partly this is to do with its misty history, partly to do with language and taxonomy, and partly to do with the wide and intricate range of species and varieties, spontaneous mutations, cultivated hybrids and crosses that typify the clan.

There have been numerous attempts at classification. Two of the most notable took opposing approaches: the American botanist Walter Tennyson Swingle lumped similar types together and gave them one species name; T. Tanaka looked at every slight variation and 'split' them into differently named species. More recently, David Mabberley has gained wide acceptance for a new classification of edible citrus into three species: citron (*Citrus medica*), merril pomelo (*C. maxima*) and blanco mandarin (*C. reticulata*).[1]

In this system, grapefruit (*C. paradisi*) is a cross between the pomelo and sweet orange; lemons (*C. limon*) derive from the citron and sour orange; and limes (*C. aurantifolia*) appear to be a hybrid of papeda, an Asian citrus fruit, and citron. Pomelo crossed with mandarin produced both sour (*C. aurantium*) and sweet oranges (*C. sinensis*), each inheriting more features of one parent than the other.

In 2012, a Chinese team uncovered the genome sequence of the sweet orange, a move they hope will improve citrus traits such as colour, taste, yield and disease resistance.[2]

Sour/Bitter Oranges (*C. aurantium*)

The above terms are largely interchangeable, but strictly speaking 'sour' refers to the acidity of the flesh, and 'bitter' to the essential oils. The trees are compact and upright with long, dark green leaves and in appropriate conditions have an extraordinary ability to survive with no care at all. Some trees in Spain are said to be over 600 years old.

Typically, the blossom is highly aromatic and the fruit radiant red-orange with thick, dimpled skin, a large petiole (leafstalk), abundant seeds and an astringent taste. It is used as a rootstock as well as in marmalade. The principal variety grown is the Seville. In Japan and China it is known as *daidai* and *taitai* respectively and has a more dwarfish habit. High in pectin, it is the citrus of choice for marmalade, and the UK supply comes almost totally from Spain around February each year. Oddly, it seems almost impossible to buy bitter oranges

Vincenzo Leonardi, *Sour Orange, Flowering Twigs and Fruits*, 1640, watercolour.

in Seville itself, the principal producing area, although I have picked them from the roadside.

In the nineteenth century, 23 varieties of bitter orange were described in Europe.[3] Today, the most prominent sub-species are the bergamot, grown in Calabria for the rind oil used in perfume, Earl Grey tea and candied peel, and the myrtle leaf or chinotto, traditionally crystallized whole in Provençal towns such as Apt, and used in the Italian soda of that name as well as in Campari.[4]

Intriguing relatives include bizzarria (an eye-catching bi-colour, intermingling or 'chimera' of bitter orange and either lemon or citron); the bouquetier types (used in neroli oils and perfumes); corniculata (with a strange, raised 'horn'); and fasciata (striped yellow and orange).

The Seville is also called *bigarade* in French, a name that overlaps with another variety, the bittersweet (*C. aurantium var. bigaradia*), which lives up to its name and is notable for its lack of acidity.

Bergamot oranges with peeled skin. The pith and peel of the bergamot is particularly thick and the latter yields a spicy-sweet essential oil much used in perfumery.

Sweet Oranges (*C. sinensis*)

The *capo* of the citrus family. No other is so widely grown and used except, arguably, in the Far East where mandarins still rule. It is the second most commonly cultivated fruit in the world, eclipsed only by the banana. The plant scientist Robert Willard Hodgson divided the category into four: common, sugar/acidless, navel and blood.[5]

There are scores of major and minor 'common' oranges, new and old. It seems a rather belittling name, although they also used to be (and sometimes still are) referred to as white or blonde to distinguish them from the blood orange.

The Valencia is the world's most important commercial orange, with large, vigorous trees suitable for a wide range of climates and soils. Late to mature, the prolific, thin-skinned fruit is virtually seedless (although a seeded variety is grown in Brazil and Australia) and lives up to its nickname, 'The King of Juice Oranges'.

The variety probably came into Portuguese possession from China via the Azores. An English nurseryman, Thomas Rivers, catalogued it in 1865 under the name Excelsior, and subsequently supplied trees to clients in California and Florida. The name Valencia is misleading: the fruit does not originate in Valencia, Spain, as is commonly assumed, but was named in its new home of California when it was deemed to resemble a late-maturing Old World orange by a homesick Spanish visitor. The fruit became known as both Hart's tardiff and Valencia late, and then simply Valencia.

There are many sweet varieties, including hamlin (possibly the world's principal variety of very early maturing juice orange); harward late (New Zealand); kona (introduced to Hawaii in 1792), midknight (from South Africa); Parson Brown (an 'early' Florida juice orange); pera (a widely grown Brazilian

Oranges for sale at a street market in Rio, Brazil. In Brazil and other tropical countries, some oranges are ripe despite their green or greenish-yellow colour. The heat preserves the chlorophyll like a natural sunscreen, but in more temperate regions, the green skin turns orange when the weather cools.

Arabs and Jews packing oranges together in Rehovoth, Israel, 1934–9.

fruit); pineapple (grown in Florida for its fine juice); and salustiana (a comparatively new Spanish variety discovered in a convent garden).

The shamouti, Palestine Jaffa or Cyprus oval originated around 1844 near Jaffa, then part of the Ottoman Empire. It was a limb sport or mutation of the local, seedy beledi strain. The thick, leathery rind peels easily to reveal brilliant, seedless flesh with a succulent flavour. Orange exports grew from 200,000 oranges in 1845 to 38 million by 1870. In 1892, around 20,000 wooden crates were imported into Britain where they gave their name to the little chocolate and orange sponge cakes still popular today. The orange gardens have disappeared but in the alleyways of Jaffa, there is a striking sculpture by the Israeli environmental artist, Ran Morin, called *Orange Suspendu*, which makes the connection between the city, the land and the fruit. Israeli producers have sold shamouti budwood to Spanish growers who can use the Jaffa name (which is an

Israeli trademark) for this fruit. The trademark also covers other citrus and orange varieties: I have also bought Jaffa oranges grown in South Africa.

Shiranui (or dekopon) is one of the newest citrus kids on the block. The fruit is large, easy to peel and seedless with a distinctive 'topknot' that gives it its American name, sumo (in Brazil they are called *kinsei*). Developed as a Japanese tangor-mandarin hybrid, they have a persuasive aroma and a melting texture but the ridiculously expensive one I tasted in New York on their 2011 debut there had a saccharine sweetness. Although the skin looks thick and tough, it quickly bruises, so the fruit is marketed in padded boxes.

Sugar/Acidless Oranges

These oranges lack acid and have an insipid, sugary flavour enjoyed in many Arabic-speaking countries, and to a certain extent in Spain, Portugal and Italy. As a consequence they are still cultivated locally to some degree, but not exported. Vainiglia is pink-fleshed, juicy, sweet and slightly bitter.

Navel Oranges

Large and easy to peel, navel oranges have an excellent flavour; the juice is delicious when freshly squeezed but, unlike that of the Valencia, quickly becomes bitter. In *Hesperides*, a seventeenth-century compendium of 1,000 citrus varieties, the Jesuit priest Giovanni Battista Ferrarius observed: 'This orange imitates to some extent the fertility of the tree which bears it in that it struggles, though unsuccessfully, to produce the fruit upon itself.'[6] The description effectively encapsulates

'1882 – A Carload of Mammoth Navel Oranges from California', c. 1909, postcard.

the embryonic fruit-within-a-fruit and protruding 'navel' that is its essential characteristic.

There are many varieties, but the most well known is the Washington or Bahia navel; its origins are unclear but it is most likely a cross-bud variation from the Brazilian variety known as *selecta*. In the nineteenth century, a Presbyterian missionary sent twelve nursery-sized trees to the US Department of Agriculture (USDA) in Washington where they were propagated under glass. Offered to anyone who cared to give them a go, a few were supplied to Eliza Tibbets in the new colony of Riverside, California. She tended the trees carefully, reputedly using dishwater to keep them alive, and they were to become the founding fruit of the state's industry. By 1893, Riverside was the wealthiest city per capita in the U.S.

Remarkably, one of the trees was transplanted to its present location in downtown Riverside, where it survives in defiance of all passing traffic. Its job was done: the semi-arid climatic conditions of the area led to a fruit of superior

Parent Washington Navel Orange Tree, Riverside, *c.* 1902. Now a national landmark, the tree is one of two that were originally given to Eliza Tibbets in 1873, propagated from trees imported from Bahia, and from which all Washington Navel oranges in California descended.

quality and rapid commercialization, although most of the citrus groves have now relocated to the Central Valley, where land is cheaper and water more readily available.

Contemporary varieties include cara cara (a very sweet, pink-red fleshed navel discovered in Venezuela); fukumoto (introduced into California from Japan); lane late (a late-maturing Australian fruit); navelate (paler than Washington with a less prominent navel); and navelina (an early-maturing fruit mostly grown in Spain), plus a whole raft of more recent late-maturing navel orange selections from Australia.

A couple of Californian companies such as LoBue Citrus and Sky Valley continue to grow heirloom navel oranges on trees planted in the 1930s. They have an excellent flavour, but are limited in supply.

Blood Oranges

A romantic but unlikely story links blood oranges with the Crusades; more probably the thorny trees were a seventeenth-century mutation originating in Sicily and, possibly, Malta. James Saunt suggests,[7] however, that they are, like navel oranges, indigenous to China. In 2012, scientists identified the anthocyanin pigment gene (nicknamed Ruby) that makes blood oranges 'bloody'.[8] The pigment is associated with cardiovascular health, but only comes out in the fruit's flesh when grown in places with extremes of sun and cold. Certain areas of Sicily provide just the right conditions – and researchers also found evidence that one blood orange variety arose independently in China.[9]

Wherever, and however, they originate – heaven, perhaps – they are the most captivating of fruit. Their aesthetic shadings are marvels of natural beauty, matched by an equally distinctive fragrance and ambrosial berry taste. Part of their allure and fascination is the fact that each one displays slightly different, marbled combinations of skin, flesh and juice pigmentation and colouring. The variations are endless, even from fruit from the same tree, picked on the same day.

'Sanguine', a languorous Jacques Prévert poem, alludes to the inherent sexual appeal of the fruit but, more prosaically, in the past their lack of uniformity has meant they have not fitted the standardization demanded by the mass market. Thankfully, the Arancia Rossa di Sicilia is PGI protected bt the

Sliced blood orange. The Arancia Rossa di Sicilia have protected geographical status. They are utterly delicious and also boast the highest vitamin C content of all oranges in the world.

EU and comprises three varieties that can only be grown in a strictly limited area south of Mount Etna: sanguinello, moro and tarocco.

Sanguinello is an ancient variety with two derivatives, sanguinello moscata (also known as Paterno after the nearby town) and sanguinello moscata cuscuna. Moro has the flavours of ripe cherry and passion fruit and pulp of a striking hue that can vary from scarlet to burgundy or almost black. The Sicilian tarocco is, in my view, arguably the world's finest orange; the distinctive colour of the flesh is a natural mutation that needs a chilly winter to develop properly, but it has a perfect blend of raspberry-rich sweetness and acidity. It is sold under the name Volcano Oranges® in the U.S. Blood oranges are also grown in California, Texas and Florida – although whether their quality matches the Italian is a matter of opinion.

Other varieties include sanguinelli (a seedy, dark Spanish blood orange that is a derivative of doblefina, once the principal blood orange in Spain) and Maltaise sanguine (Cape Bon, near Tunis, is said to produce fruit of the highest quality – Saunt agrees with the French, who call this semi-blood variety 'Queen of Oranges').[10]

Hybrids

Citrus fruits are almost wantonly promiscuous: they reproduce easily with each other and many crosses and mutations are known, both natural and man-made, within genera as well as species. In some cases, they are self-pollinating and are also able to produce fruit and fertile seed without sexual mixing.

Citrus has always inspired the experimental. The desire to cross, breed and create new forms combines the sense of divine creation with empirical curiosity. There are constant surprises, as it does not always breed true from seed. The most effective way to ensure consistency is by grafting the selected scion onto a rootstock, a technique that has been around since ancient times. The *Geoponica*, a tenth-century Byzantine farming manual, includes instructions on how to make citrons black or red by grafting onto apple and mulberry trees respectively, and how to form them into the shape of birds, animals or human faces. Perhaps best not taken too literally, it also suggests making apples red by urinating on the tree . . .

The introduction of grafting into commercial planting in the mid- to late nineteenth century was a way of preventing disease as well as improving quality. The sour orange was the favoured rootstock until the outbreak of the *tristeza* virus. Modern innovations include *in vitro* grafting (grafting a shoot tip from a mature plant onto a seedling rootstock).

Commercial breeders aim for improved yield, better storage qualities, attractive appearance and tastier flavours, but the goal of another group, often amateurs, is to produce a frost-hardy citrus plant with sweet, edible fruit. It is said that such growers usually start with *Poncirus trifoliata*, a deciduous, cold-resistant citrus relative, and invariably fail in their endeavours. Nature still rules, OK.

Various hybrids have become fully fledged members of the citrus family. Tangors are a mandarin (tangerine) and sweet orange cross, with varieties such as temple, dweet, Ellendale, umatilla and murcott. The latter has such thin peel, it is clipped, rather than pulled, from the tree. Juicy and complex with a pockmarked skin and brief season, temples are believed to have come from the West Indies to Florida early in the twentieth century. Ortaniques, sometimes called honey tangerines, are natural tangors, reputedly found on Jamaica around 1920. Mineolas are often thought by the public to be oranges, although they are a cross between tangerines and grapefruit: the offspring provide a good illustration of how cross-breeding can produce an unexpectedly rich, tart and aromatic result.

The naming of hybrids is as romantic and alluring as the complexity of the fruit itself. Ambersweet is part orange, clementine, mandarin and grapefruit; volkamer a lemon-sour orange hybrid that originated in Italy. Chironja is a sweet orange and grapefruit cross found as a wild seedling in Puerto Rico, eaten like a grapefruit but sweeter and brighter. Citrange is a cross between a sweet orange and *Poncirus trifoliata*: when crossed in turn with a kumquat, the result is the magnificently named citrangequat – one can see why the whole business soon becomes so bewitching and bewildering.

Citrology can become a magnificent obsession. In his time at the Taiwan Agricultural Research Institute, Huang Ah-hsien developed around 170 different varieties, but his last project before retirement in 2012 was to breed the world's largest orange – The King. It is said to weigh 600g on average, and is as wide as your face. It is seemingly more mega-mandarin than supersized orange, but it has nonetheless gained its creator, known by his students as the 'God of Citrus', a place in citrus history.

4

Business and Trade

Oranges have circled the world in the wake of wars, conquest, trade and botanical quests. The market is still dominated by the established producers, but new orange-growing countries are springing up from Swaziland to Cuba. Citrus commerce may be founded on a gift from the gods, but business is business. And oranges are big business, indeed.

For centuries, scarcity and cost restricted them to the households of the aristocracy and bourgeoisie. The two main factors that brought the fruit within reach of the middle, then the working classes were the development of steam power and the invention of artificial refrigeration.

The American fashion for citrus in the nineteenth century spurred the export of oranges from Sicily's legendary Conca d'Oro valley, a move that was intriguingly bound up with the history of the Mafia. In the mid-1880s, according to John Dickie, 'an astonishing 2.5 million cases of Italian citrus fruit arrived in New York every year, most of them from Palermo'.[1]

The California and Florida citrus industries, however, were soon to speed ahead as trade was boosted by the building of the railroads, improved shipping, new agricultural and plant-breeding techniques, irrigation advances and innovative marketing ideas – not to mention sheer, hard labour.

A train comes through the orange groves in Florida, 1910–20. The coming of the railroads was crucial to the rapid development of the citrus industry, enabling growers to send fruit quickly and efficiently across the country.

In 1886, the Wolfskill orchards sent the first train carrying nothing but oranges from California to the East Coast, but as the century came to a close, the Californian industry faced major problems: a land boom, oversupply, domination by the railroad powers and pest blight. The growers could not afford to destroy the orchards, but they couldn't stop the fruit ripening either. To gain more bargaining power, they set up co-operatives such as the California Fruit Growers Exchange (CFGE). The problem was that they either had to find a way of storing the fruit or make people eat more. Advertising was the answer, and in the process of building mass consumption of this 'new' and 'fresh' fruit, they also sold California as the quintessential sunshine state.

Business boomed, helped by an increased awareness of nutrition; oranges were sold as a cure for all ills. By the end of the 1920s, Californian citrus farmers earned four times the average American income. Riverside became a swanky town of grand mansions and parks, and the CFGE expanded

Scenes among the orange growers in Orange County, Florida, 1885, black and white photoprint.

Orange Ball display at California Orange Week, c. 1938. The annual festival of the citrus industry was one of the social events of the year.

into a huge, vertically integrated industry with its own forests to provide timber for the crates. They even had international sales offices. In 1907, they launched their own brand, Sunkist, a first for fresh fruit, and poured money into marketing. The catchphrase was 'Oranges for Health, California for Wealth'.

Gradually, however, overproduction again became a problem. To regulate the price, 'golden mountains' of surplus oranges were destroyed, a shocking act during the Depression that was powerfully denounced by John Steinbeck in *The Grapes of Wrath* (1939).

The mild, sunny climate of the West Coast suits the production of navel oranges; by contrast, Valencias do better in the sandy soil and hot, damp climate of Florida. Family juice stands once flourished there like flocks of flamingos along

Freda Jones of Portland, Oregon, picking oranges, 1954.

the state highways, especially in the Indian River region. Thousands have disappeared since the 1960s, victims of disasters, diseases, commercial development and the pressures of a big, globalized industry.

In the commercial golden age of citrus, the fruit was packed in crates with brilliant labels or even individually wrapped in coloured tissue paper. As oranges morphed from luxury item to daily staple, taste became a lesser priority, however, against the need for consistency, conformity and good looks. Before long the model of co-operative settler communities would be replaced by mega-corporations and big business.

Developments in cold storage and maritime transport enabled the southern hemisphere to enter the export market, so the north could enjoy the classic fruit of winter year round. Brazil, particularly the state of São Paulo, is the world's largest producer of oranges, most of which are processed for juice. Per hectare, it is more profitable than coffee or wheat. Large-scale production and logistics underpin the Brazilian success, but the pressure for low costs has led to dubious practices in the past. A study in 1999 found growers in Brazil (also Chile and Ecuador) hired underage labourers to pick the oranges.[2] The situation did improve over the following decade, but a further report in November 2010 recognized that although

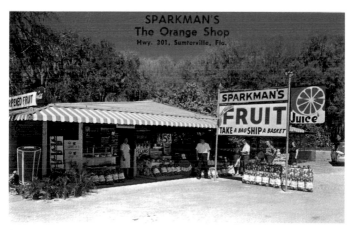

Sparkman's Orange Shop, Sumterville, Florida, 1950s. Mom 'n' pop businesses offered fresh fruit and juice to tourists. The fruit could also be shipped north as gift baskets.

former president Lula da Silva had made significant efforts to reduce extreme poverty and child labour, 'The issue still remains urgent . . . Especially in the poorer northeastern part of the country, many children have no choice but to become integrated into the illegal job market.'[3]

Not that adult workers necessarily fare much better. In 2006, Brazilian unions estimated that 40 per cent of the 60,000 orange pickers in São Paulo earned less than the minimum wage, and half did not receive legally required benefits.[4] The issue, however, is not unique to South America, and despite experiments with picking machines (the drawback is they can only be used on trees where the whole crop ripens simultaneously) hand-picking remains the best way to harvest, particularly for table oranges.

An old slogan for the Florida Citrus Commission claimed that 'A day without orange juice is like a day without sunshine', but in the land of opportunity the reality of agricultural labour is often far from sunny. A poem of 1961, 'The Orange Picker' by David Ignatow, is a disenchanted juxtaposition of the heraldic orange banner of the groves seen from afar compared to the hard, close-up reality of picking them – 'these oranges have failed me'. The campaigns by labour leader and civil rights activist César Chávez led to numerous improvements for Latino farmworkers in California, but the issue of illegal migrants, victims of harsh conditions and substandard wages, remains contentious as the recent documentary film *La Cosecha* (The Harvest, 2011) forcibly demonstrated.

In 2003, an investigation by a Florida newspaper found migrant workers were paid only 3.5 cents per half-gallon of fresh juice that typically retailed for $3.39.[5] In the citrus groves, as in many other parts of u.s. agriculture, it's often a race to the bottom for a cheaper production process, especially in an industry squeezed by imports, increased costs and falling

Picking oranges, 1902. In the early days of the industry, harvesters climbed ladders and pulled the fruits off by hand, putting them into pails or shoulder sacks. Clippers were introduced in 1900.

demand. Balancing immigration controls and workers' rights with the need for labour remains a tricky goal.

The Coalition of Immokalee Workers (CIW) argues that there is a continuum of systematic abuse that ranges from 'sweatshop' conditions, including sub-poverty wages, no right to overtime pay, and no right to organize, through to

A migrant
orange picker,
Polk County,
Florida, 1937.

'modern-day slavery' with captive farmworkers held against their will through threats and even the actual use of violence. Their travelling museum documents the appalling present-day conditions of slave labourers: astonishingly, since the mid-1990s more than 1,000 slaves have been freed in at least six cases in Florida.[6]

Equally, the CIW point to the responsibility of agribusiness in controlling the 'demand' side of the U.S. produce market,

> the major food-buying corporations that profit from the artificially-low cost of U.S. produce picked by workers in sweatshop and, in the worst cases, slavery conditions.

Ultimately, those modern mega corporations must leverage their vast resources and market influence as major produce buyers to clean up slavery and other labor abuses in their supply chains once and for all.

A recent investigation into the squalid living conditions of citrus workers in Calabria also alleged that African migrant labourers were earning very low wages picking oranges to supply juice concentrates to multinational companies. The price of oranges was so low, it was reported, that many farmers left their crops to rot on the tree.[7]

There are other problems: frost at the wrong time of the year, for example, can be seriously damaging. Burners or 'smudge pots' have been used to heat the groves on frosty nights, and some growers use giant fans to mix the cold low air with the warmer air above. Another method of heating is to turn on the water sprinklers: as long as freezing water is in contact with the fruit, its temperature cannot fall below zero, since the water releases heat as it freezes. This works for a short-lived cold snap, but if it stays below freezing, the

Florida Modern Slavery Museum truck. The museum consists of a cargo truck outfitted as a replica of those involved in a 21st-century slavery operation, developed in consultation with workers who have escaped from forced labour conditions.

Oscar Lewis spraying the orange grove, Lakeland, Florida.

oranges will freeze too. Other strategies, according to the University of Arizona, include covering small trees, stringing the trees with lights and maintaining soil moisture, as well as care in initial variety, rootstock and site selection.[8]

Disease is also a constant concern: fruit flies can devastate an industry, and 'citrus greening' spread by the Asian citrus psyllid poses a particular nightmare scenario.[9] The disease, named after the sour, green, misshapen fruit it gives rise to, has devastated millions of acres of citrus crops in the u.s. and elsewhere. It entered Florida early in the twenty-first century, and recent data showed that 18 per cent of trees were infected, with the rate doubling annually.[10] Despite strict controls and quarantine regulations, in March 2012, the deadly citrus disease was detected in Los Angeles County in a residential neighbourhood, probably introduced via an illegally imported bud. There is currently no confirmed cure to a problem that has been described as akin to trying to get rid of the mosquito, although the industry is pouring millions into research.

Management and containment of the problem includes constant inspection, removal of infected trees and control of the insects, each no bigger than the head of a pin, which spread the virus. As a result, some farmers douse their crops with a heavy wash of pesticide or 'nutritional spray programs' which, Evan Fraser and Andrew Rimas warn, could 'turn the environment into a poisonous morass',[11] and leaves infected trees in place. On the other hand, some farmers believe that higher crop yields have been an unexpected side benefit of the enhanced foliar nutrition.

Chemicals may provide one remedy, but not every grower wants to use more of them – and scientists are now rethinking the efficacy of such a 'scorched earth' tree destruction policy. One strategy has been to establish new varieties of oranges and trees; scientists at Cornell are working on genetically engineering a tree that shows resistance to the virus.[12] In Texas, work is advancing on genetic modification using spinach genes.[13] The University of Florida is evaluating silver mulch as a shiny, visually disruptive control, and in California, tiny, stingless parasitic wasps have been released into the environment as a natural enemy of the psyllid.[14]

From the consumer's standpoint, however, buying organic oranges is the best way to ensure that the fruit has been cultivated without pesticides or dyes that match the fruit to our mental image of the ideal orange.[15] Fairtrade oranges offer a small but fast-growing niche market: in South Africa, for example, there are over twenty producers who grow certified citrus. So, when in doubt, buy Fairtrade juice – or squeeze your own from organic Fairtrade oranges.

The trade in oranges and orange juice is interlinked. We take it for granted, but it was not always the case.

5
Orange Juice

'Is the orange juice fresh?', I asked a waitress in a Liverpool restaurant. 'Oh, yes,' she replied, 'I've just opened the packet.'

It is easy to laugh at this story, and equally easy to identify with it. The orange is both a fruit to eat – and to drink. Think fruit juice, think orange juice, and the word 'fresh' is not far behind. It is the most popular processed juice in the world, and although sales may have dipped in recent years as a result of a slow economy, poor harvests, rising prices and alternative options, many think breakfast *sans* OJ is no breakfast at all.

Writer and historian Margaret Visser describes drinking the juice of a fruit as a quite different experience from that of eating it: '[It is] the refined and luxurious essence of the thing, produced by previously performed fastidious effort, like de-boned chicken or strained consommé.'[1] Alas, such an exquisite homage to the fruit of the Hesperides has been lost in the thickets of urban Tetrapacks.

Orange juice has travelled a long way in every sense. Constantly reinventing itself, it has gone from a product of nature to a global industrial commodity, traded on the New York Stock Exchange, and even shot into outer space as powdered Tang.

Margaret Thatcher drinking orange juice on 6 October 1983, the morning after the midnight revelation that Trade and Industry Secretary Cecil Parkinson was to be the father of his secretary's baby.

Most commercial juices appear to tell a story that suggest they're nothing more than squeezed fruit poured into the packet. Yet the mass-market product is standardized, industrialized and globalized. Unlike the description by John McPhee of how the colour of the fresh juice he bought at Penn Station each morning deepened over the seasons,[2] the reality is a tale of technical wizardry and marketing savvy. When it comes to the dark arts of advertising, freshness is relative: the only truly fresh juice is the one you squeeze yourself.

A drop in the price of West Indian sugar in the seventeenth century opened up the consumption in Paris of lemonade. Orangeade followed but was less popular, and *limonade* became the general term for all drinks made of sugar water and aromatic scents such as jasmine, mace, carnations and orange blossom.

Always one to spot a trend, Pepys recorded how he drank a pint of orange juice in 1669: 'they drink the juice as wine, with sugar, and it is a very fine drink; but, it being new, I was doubtful whether it might not do me hurt.' A little later, another popular drink, *orgeat*, made with almonds and orange-flower water, became a favourite in eighteenth-century London refreshment houses and pleasure gardens.

However, it was another 200 years until the idea of marketing orange juice commercially was put into practice – in California. When growers facing a glut began to cut down trees, Sunkist came up with the sensationally successful slogan 'Drink an Orange'. Residue waste was used for by-products such as cattle feed, but sales would never have grown without other factors: efficient distribution by railroad and truck, the increased perception of orange juice as nutritious and the introduction of the flash pasteurization process to prolong shelf life.

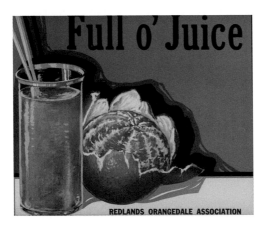

Redlands Orangedale Association, Full o' Juice crate poster, early 20th century.

The bulk processed market, however, was really created in Florida in the first half of the twentieth century, when they began seriously to pulp, reduce and first can, then freeze the plentiful fruit to sell year-round as FCOJ (frozen concentrate orange juice). It became hugely profitable, subsequently spurred on also by the need to supply vitamin C to the troops in the thick of the Second World War.

Growers and producers had to deal with a very different problem in the 1970s, however, when severe frosts ruined harvests. The Florida Department of Citrus decided to support the relatively new industry in Brazil to ensure a source of supply. Growth was phenomenal: there may be an awful lot of coffee in Brazil, but now there is an awful lot of orange juice as well. Brazil is the world's largest OJ producer, and most is exported.

Today, unless it expressly says so on the label, a carton of Florida packed juice is unlikely to have come from 100 per cent U.S. oranges. Concentrate juice will probably be a blend of Floridian, Brazilian, Mexican and others. In 2012, however, there were signs that this situation was changing when PepsiCo announced that it was returning to using only oranges from Florida in its Tropicana Pure Premium juices. Nonetheless, for every five glasses of orange juice consumed worldwide, it has been estimated that three are produced in Brazil, a figure which is unlikely to change dramatically.[3] As Saudi Arabia is to oil, Brazil is to OJ.

Brazil has succeeded through efficiency, extensive planting, technological know-how and integrated supply chains. In the early 1990s, the four biggest Brazilian processors acquired plants in Florida. A decade later, they controlled nearly half the processing capacity in the state. As Jason Clay has written, 'The expansion of the Brazilian orange processing industry into Florida has been very calculating.'[4]

In 2002, the Brazilian citrus industry moved into NFC (Not From Concentrate) juice, a sector developed years earlier in Florida. It was a sign of things to come. In Santos, São Paolo, Citrosuco now operates the largest OJ terminal in the world, from which they export premium NFC juice and bulk FCOJ (cheaper to transport as it takes up less space), as well as one in Ghent, Belgium, which is the first in the world to receive and distribute bulk aseptic NFC. When the first shipment was made in 1999 it was hailed as a new era in the ocean transport of juice.

For over 70 years, the Florida citrus industry was protected from overseas competition by financial barriers, but the state's Equalization Tax was discontinued in 2003, and in 2011 an anti-dumping challenge on U.S. tariff duties was settled by the WTO in favour of Brazil. A year later, however, Florida Citrus Mutual, the country's largest citrus grower organization, filed a petition to reinstate the duty.[5] Another row broke out when Florida growers claimed that Brazil was circumventing duty by shipping their product first to Canada, then to the U.S. The year 2011 also saw a merger approved between the giant Citrovita and Citrosuco groups in a bid for them to become the world's largest wholesale supplier of orange juice.

The impact all this is likely to have on the Florida industry is uncertain; some have predicted it will be crushed, others that it will be hurt (especially small producers) but not destroyed. Early in 2012, global consumer confidence was damaged by controversy surrounding the use of the fungicide Carbendazim in exported Brazilian orange juice. The fungicide is used in limited quantities in Europe, but the U.S. banned its use in 2009. Domestic juice producers in the U.S. attempted to use the scare to their advantage but, as Brazilian oranges make up around 85 per cent of global exports, prices sky-rocketed.[6] In response to u.s. concerns, Brazil subsequently announced that it too was dropping use of the chemical on its citrus crops.

The past decade has also seen a search for new and non-saturated markets such as Asia, as a result of population growth and increased prosperity, and the Middle East because of their ban on alcohol. Poorer populations tend to drink juice they squeeze themselves or simply to eat the whole fruit.[7] As incomes rise, they drink more concentrate, then more not-from-concentrate – and ironically are likely to come full circle by squeezing their own increasingly expensive but fresh oranges. Or, rather, by having someone else squeeze the fruit for them.

The juice-making process used to be perfectly straightforward. You cut and squeezed a fresh orange . . . so why has it become so complicated and confusing?

Until the end of the nineteenth century, kitchen squeezers were made in two parts with long handles, one bowl-shaped, the other domed, joined by hinges. The squeezer we recognize today, with ribs, juice-filtering rim and teeth for catching the pips, first appeared in the American Sears Roebuck catalogue of 1897. Although initially sold as a lemon squeezer, as Margaret Visser commented, it was a brilliantly simple design based on the power of the human hand when twisted. She added,

> The squeezer began its conquest of the world's kitchen when an advertisement was placed in the Saturday Evening Post for 19 February 1916 suggesting that we should 'Drink an Orange' for breakfast, and offering round glass orange-squeezers to readers for ten cents each.[8]

In time, electric mixers came with orange-juicing attachments – the trick was to hold the orange still while the mixer did the twisting. Today there are all sorts of fancy devices and machines, including Philippe Starck's tarantula-like Alessi squeezer, but I think an old-fashioned wooden reamer with a ridged, convex blade remains one of the best and cheapest juicers you can buy, as long as you don't mind sticky fingers.

The acid and natural sugar levels of oranges are measured in units called Brix, and heavy fruits with well-coloured juice high in sugar, as is characteristic of the best Florida oranges, are the most valuable. The taste and texture of oranges, however, naturally differs by type, season, location and even the position on the tree. This innate variation may be part of the attraction to an individual consumer, but it is also the last thing an industrialized product needs.

As freshly squeezed juice lasts only a short time, the growers considered how to preserve the juice. The first step was canning, but canned juice initially tasted terrible. Vacuum-evaporated concentrate was first frozen in Florida in the 1920s but the flavour was lost when the water was removed. The incentive to produce a quality frozen juice was strongly motivated, as has been noted, by the need to supply the troops with provisions during the Second World War. It was a formidable technical and practical challenge. The u.s. army could hardly transport vast quantities of fruit to millions of soldiers; the logistics were impossible. The first solution was powdered orange juice – all the soldier had to do was add water. Unfortunately, it tasted so bad that no one could then drink the stuff. Canned juice, on the other hand, was bulky and heavy to transport long distances and the metal was needed for the war effort.

All efforts were directed to the development of a better frozen juice concentrate. Finally, scientists at the Florida Citrus

Visitors sampling some Florida orange juice at the Highlands Hotel, Ocala, Florida, *c.* 1950s.

Commission made a big leap forward in 1943 when they discovered that the taste of the concentrate could be improved by the addition of a small amount of fresh juice before it was frozen. It was easier to ship than large cans of juice and when reconstituted, you could almost believe you were drinking the former. It changed the history of orange juice forever.

From then on, the growth of the giant Tropicana and Minute Maid brands were built on the post-war baby boom and the rise of the suburban lifestyle, in which the act of peeling an orange was considered time-wasting and tedious, as well as new kitchen innovations: refrigerators, frozen dinners and those iconic little tins of FCOJ.

The process is at once fundamentally simple and highly complex. The fruit is washed and sorted, and the peel pricked

Woman pouring Orange Nip frozen orange juice for her children in Sarasota, Florida, 1963. Many Americans grew up on reconstituted juice made by diluting the thawed concentrate with water. In the UK in the 1960s, it was sold by Findus; there was even a pop song called 'Frozen Orange Juice' that offered a vision of continental sophistication.

to extract oil. The juicing machines strip off the pith and peel and extract the juice, which goes to a 'finishing' screen where the pulp and seeds are removed. The waste is variously used for livestock feed, pectin or brewing. The scale of operations today is immense; orange juice flows like a mighty river. The scientist Pierre Laszlo makes an apt comparison with an oil refinery.[9]

For FCOJ, the juice is concentrated into a kind of slurry by evaporation, cooled, pasteurized and frozen, often for many months. Once filtered water is added, it becomes Ready-To-Serve (RTS).

Coca-Cola introduced Minute Maid chilled juice reconstituted from frozen concentrate onto the market in 1973. Their claim was that the process allowed better blending and elimination of seasonal variations in the orange crop, thus producing a drink of consistent quality.

Tropicana (Pepsi-Cola), on the other hand, went into the so-called 'Orange Juice Wars' in the 1980s with their brilliant Not From Concentrate (NFC) concept, originally devised 30 years earlier. The genius of the idea was that consumers were willing to pay more for the extra value.[10] NFC is juice that has been pasteurized and 'de-aerated' to prevent oxidization. Sometimes held in tanks for many months before packaging, the juice is often 'adjusted' to meet customer specifications. If it is too sour, pale or watery, for example, 'flavour packs' of orange-derived essences can be used to restore uniformity.

U.S. legislation also allows the addition of up to 10 per cent mandarin juice to improve the colour. 'Bits', or the

A Tropicana truck in Bradenton, Florida. Now owned by PepsiCo, Tropicana was founded in 1947 by a Sicilian immigrant named Anthony T. Rossi. He later invented a pasteurization process that enabled him to mass market chilled, not-from-concentrate juice in waxed paper cartons.

preposterously named 'juicy bits', often derived from altogether different oranges from the original juice, may also be added back to both RTS and NFC juice.

Interestingly, and ironically, in 2012 PepsiCo announced a plan to sell more of its Tropicana-brand OJ – by adding water. Less juice means higher profit margins, especially if you package it in innovative wrapping.[11]

Early in 2012, a class-action suit was filed by a California mother against Tropicana alleging that their NFC Pure Premium juice is in fact 'heavily processed' and not a 'natural' product. Shortly afterwards, Coca-Cola's 'Simply Orange' was the target of similar litigation. The argument is that the addition of aromas and flavour packs 'change the essential nature' of the juice; the case goes to the heart of whether juice-making is an art or a science, and what is or is not natural.[12]

'Fresh', 'pure' and even 'natural' are slippery words. However, super-premium 'freshly squeezed juice' is unpasteurized, processed and delivered within 24 hours. Other premium juices are partially pasteurized and need refrigeration even before opening. Both can be expensive, but are the latter worth it? In 2008, *Cooks Illustrated* magazine in the U.S. reported, 'The reality is they undergo many of the same processes as any bottled OJ – and can also be "doctored" to improve their flavour.'

Changes to EU regulations in 2012 confirmed a distinction between fresh juice and concentrated juice, and banned the addition of sugar or sweeteners to fruit juices, but in the UK so-called 'juice drinks' have no legal definitions, only marketplace ones. In the U.S., a blend of juice with other ingredients such as high-fructose corn syrup is called a juice drink or juice cocktail. The fruit content can vary enormously. It is quite possible for a bottle to contain only a tiny amount of juice in the ingredients list of water, sugar, flavourings, sweeteners and colourings, like soda pop with a fruity flavour (see chapter Nine).

UK fruit nectar drinks must contain at least 25–50 per cent juice depending on the fruit and if it contains concentrate, this must be stated. In the US, nectar is a diluted juice that contains fruit juice or purée, water and usually artificial sweeteners.

Confusion also arises between the terms 'orange flavour' and 'orange flavoured': only with the latter can you get at least a tiny amount of the named fruit. Juice drinks continue to be highly popular with the industry (and thus marketed heavily to the consumer) as they are cheaper than pure juice to produce and cushion the impact of all the industrial headaches such as freezing crops, poor yields, exchange rate volatility and supermarket price pressures.

A single serving of one particular juice drink, The Parents Jury in the UK discovered in 2003, contained over four teaspoons of sugar (sometimes listed as 'carbohydrate'). The use of fruit pictures and descriptions on nutritionally poor products, they also contended, was highly misleading.[13]

Then, there are squashes and cordials, fruit-based syrups of varying strengths that have to be diluted. Carbonated beverages such as pop, soda or fizzy drinks contain (at the minimum) carbonated water, sweeteners and, perhaps, even some fruit juice.

If I were an orange, I'd sue.

6

Blossom, Zest and Peel

Despite all commercialization, adulteration and debasement, the orange retains its power to enchant, especially the scent of orange blossom. It can fly you to the moon on gossamer wings, and is one of the most alluring fragrances in the world, signifying romance and sensuality.

In 1663, Jan Anthonisz. van Ravesteyn painted the Princess of Ligne wearing an exquisite diadem of pearls and imitation orange blossoms of costly enamel. It is unclear whether this composed noblewoman, barely visible above an outsize ruff and laden with strings of pearls, is entering into the state of marriage, but the fashion for highly perfumed orange-blossom bridal bouquets and head-dresses was certainly growing in Europe by the late seventeenth century. In the painting *Still-life with Turkey Pie* by Pieter Claesz (1627), the decorative bird holds an orange blossom in its beak to signify a marital theme, as does the sprig on top of a brioche in Jean-Siméon Chardin's *The Brioche* (1763).

The fashion for orange blossom was firmly established in Europe by the nineteenth century. Even America became enthralled by it: Ann Monsarrat tells the soap opera tale of Miss Mary Hellen,

Wedding wreath, 1854. The orange blossom is made from dyed feathers mounted on silk-wrapped wire, trimmed with silk ribbons.

a badly behaved young lady who trifled with the affections of all three sons of President John Quincy Adams before settling for the middle one, [who] wore orange blossoms for her White House wedding in Washington in the winter of 1828, when, according to her cousin and bridesmaid, Abigail Adams, she 'looked very handsome in white satin, orange blossoms and pearls'.[1]

In 1840 Queen Victoria wore a wreath of fragrant orange-flower blossoms over her lace wedding veil instead of a diamond tiara: white flowers for virginity, orange for fecundity was the connotation. Such was the general demand that orange blossom was transported north from Provence in barrels containing alternate layers of flowers and salt. Flowers were even imported to Europe from Florida.

It all became too much. By the 1870s, one arbiter of good taste in England, John Cordy Jeaffreson, was begging for a change from the 'colourless crown', stating 'not one lovely girl in a thousand could wear without disadvantage the solely yellow-white orange-flowers', suggesting they 'brighten their wreaths with green, purple, red and crimson'. His objection was not merely aesthetic:

> Custom and romance have raised the chaplet of orange-blossoms to unmerited respect. The white of the orange-flower is an impure white, and the symbolism of the plant is a reason why some other flower should be adopted by the English bride.[2]

His plea, however, fell on deaf female ears, with waxy imitations increasingly replacing the real thing.

Woman boarding the 'Orange Blossom Special' train, Sebring, Florida, 1930s. This passenger train ran between New York City and Miami and was renowned for luxury and speed. In winter, a section also went to Tampa and St Petersburg. It was inaugurated in 1925, suspended during the Second World War, and had its last run in 1953.

The scent is more than beguiling, it is valuable. When the flowers are distilled, they yield an essential oil with an intoxicating, slightly fruity and fresh floral scent. Citrus oil can be obtained from the peel, leaves and twigs of the fruit, as well as the buds and flowers. Depending on whether bitter, bittersweet or sweet oranges are used, the flavour profile and key notes will vary subtly.

The finest neroli oil, distilled from bitter orange buds and flowers, is lightly astringent and spicy. It is said to be named after the princess of Nerola in Italy, who used it to perfume her gloves and bath. So-called petitgrain oils are obtained by distillation of leaves and small branches. Less expensive oils, used as flavourings by the food industry, are made by steam distillation, solvent extraction or supercritical fluid systems from the pulp and peel left over from industrial juice extraction.

Orange-flower water remains after the oil is removed by steam distillation. It is highly popular in Middle Eastern and Mediterranean areas for medical and household purposes, and to perfume pastries and sweet syrups. In the fourteenth century, Boccaccio in the *Decameron* highlighted the natural affinity with moments of wanton dalliance when he described the bedchamber of a Sicilian harlot in Naples as perfumed with rose and orange water and other costly scents.

In 1453, the Duke of Burgundy gave a banquet in Lille: in the centre of the table was a 'subtlety', a representation of the Castle of Lusignan with the legendary Queen Melisinda, half woman, half serpent, seated at the summit of the tower, while the moat was filled with orange-blossom water issuing from fountains in the outer walls.

New World chocolate and Old World oranges were an intercontinental flavour marriage waiting to happen. Reputedly, on cold, dreary days Marie Antoinette would call

Orange-blossom wedding favour, 1889, made from wax, cloth, paper and silk satin ribbon on wire.

for hot chocolate infused with orange-blossom water and sweet almonds. The story also goes that after she complained to court pharmacist Sulpice Debauve about the unpleasant taste of her medicine, he devised a novel way of combining the latter with cocoa, sugar and flavourings in a pill or coin-shaped form. She named the coin-shaped chocolates *pistoles*, and they are still sold by the confectioners Debauve & Gallais – *sans medecin*.

Orange-blossom honey is produced by placing beehives in the citrus groves, which also helps pollination; it is highly prized for its delicate but seductive taste. In the markets of Iran you can find baskets of dried orange blossom, and a speciality of the Caspian littoral is a delicate preserve of transparent bitter orange blossoms.[3]

Orange-blossom perfume, Florida, 1946.

Little goes to waste in an orange. Julia F. Morton described how South Sea Islanders traditionally used crushed fruit and maccrated leaves as soap. William Safford, the first governor of Guam, recorded seeing women standing in a river rubbing clothing with sour orange pulp before scrubbing them with corncobs.[4] And an article in the *California Citrograph* in 1931 reported that snuff boxes that looked like light buckskin were still being crafted from sun-dried orange hemispheres in Acireale, Sicily.

The art of candying peel came to Europe with the Arabs, along with sugar cane. Conserved either dry or in syrup, the sweetmeats became known in Britain as 'succades' or 'suckets'. They even had their own cutlery: a small two-pronged fork at one end of the handle and a teaspoon-sized bowl at the other. In the eighteenth century, Mrs Mary Eales gives a 'receipt' for 'China Chips' in which the rind is 'cut in long chips, but very thin, with none of the White'. Although she uses China oranges, she adds, '*Sevil* would do the same Way, if you like them with a little Sugar, and very bitter'.[5]

There are recipes for candied zest, peel, oranges and liquors using both China oranges and Sevilles in the English cookbook *The Complete Confectioner* (1800) by Hannah Glasse and Maria Wilson. Interestingly, they add,

> The quintessence of those sorts of fruits cannot be drawn here as in the countries that produce them; because, besides that they lose so much of their primitive flavour by importation, the price they fetch in this country renders it an impossible thing for the distiller to think of drawing that quintessence from them with any profit or advantage to himself.[6]

The practice of mixing orange juice with wine is said to have been enjoyed by the ancient Chinese, and in the late Byzantine period there was an intriguing Cypriot custom of stopping wine and water carafes with bitter oranges.[7] Hyper-realist, seventeenth-century Dutch still-life paintings show a whole orange or lemon with the skin half-peeled in a helical strip but still attached, placed in an enormous wine glass like a huge Martini olive. The fruit would be immersed in wine, and the loose portion of the peel used to rub the rim of the glass before drinking. Sometimes the technique was so refined that you simply stirred the contents of a glass with a knife that had been used to scrape the peel of an orange.

The Dutch were also fond of 'bitters', a concentrated essence made by marinating dried bitter orange peel and other botanicals in alcohol, especially gin. The green peel of bitter Curaçao oranges (*C. aurantium var. curassaviensis*) is still used in the liqueur of that name as well as in some varieties of Belgian beer.

Rum shrub was an eighteenth-century concoction initially made to hide the 'flaws' in early rum. A relative of other rum-based drinks of the time such as grog and bumboo, at its simplest it is made by adding sugar and orange or lime juice to rum or brandy. Louis XIV is said to have particularly favoured a mix of orange, spirits and sugar as an aphrodisiac. However, the bartenders of old were not content to just keep things simple. There are recipes for orange shrub, tinctures, punches and cordials in William Clarke's *The Publican and Innkeeper's Practical Guide* (1830) varied enough to shame any contemporary mixologist.

Drinks such as these were sometimes given a French name, as in *Crème de fine Orange*. They were the forerunner of orange liqueurs such as Cointreau, Grand Marnier, Drambuie, the Curaçao and triple sec 'types' and many more that are, in turn, part of cocktail classics such as the Sidecar, Pegu Club and the Cosmopolitan. Orange 'country wine' is a good brew if you have enough oranges, as is Provençal *vin d'orange*, orange-flavoured wine on a wine and brandy base. Orange juice also makes a fine Campari mixer; whether you call it Buck's Fizz or mimosa, champagne and OJ is a spiffing party drink; and no holiday in southern Spain is complete without a jug of summer sangria, orange slices bobbing on top.

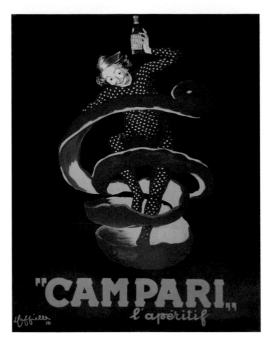

Leonetto Cappiello, Campari poster, 'Spiritello', 1921, lithograph. Campari is an alcoholic aperitif made from infusing bitter and aromatic orange peel, fruit and herbs in alcohol and water. The drink was invented by Gaspare Campari in Italy in 1860.

Experimentation with peel continues. A few years ago researchers at Cornell, using the greenhouse gas carbon dioxide, found it could make plastics. In 2011, British scientists at the University of York announced that they were setting up the Orange Peel Exploitation Company to produce chemicals, materials and fuels from orange waste leftover from juice-making.[8] And although it sounds crazy, orange oil may just be the thing to produce a more durable and longer lasting vehicle tyre. In 2012, Yokohama launched a line of tyres made with orange oil processed into a resin that gives them a better grip and tread life. No one is saying just how much orange peel it takes to produce one tyre, but it could be very good news for hard-pressed Florida growers.

And in the same spirit, green writers today suggest a multitude of individual uses for the peel: rub on light bulbs to emit fresh scent, make orange-scented cleaners or pot-pourri, soak in vodka, buff nails, discourage cats and mosquitoes . . . what a fruit!

7
The Poetry of Oranges

Enamelled green trees with courtly flowers and fruit of an eternal springtime could hardly fail to inspire centuries of poets, writers and musicians. 'A Garden of Orange Trees' by Tu-Fu (AD 712–770) delicately portrays the enchantment that comes with the blossom:

> In the full of spring on the banks of a river,
> Two big gardens planted with thousands of orange
>   trees,
> Their thick leaves are putting the clouds to shame,
> Over the wealth of their fallen blossoms one walks
>   without touching the snow.[1]

Tin-Tun-Ling's (AD 772–845) 'The Shadow of an Orange Leaf' conveys a haunting, contemporary melancholy:

> Alone, in her room, a young girl embroiders silken
>   flowers.
> Suddenly she hears a distant flute . . .
> She trembles.
> She thinks a young man is speaking to her of love.
> Through the paper window, the shadow of an orange

Kimono with a design of oranges, 1800–50, figured silk satin with embroidered and resist-dyed decoration.

leaf comes and settles on her knees . . .
She closes her eyes,
She thinks a hand is tearing her dress.[2]

The description by a twelfth-century Muslim poet of oranges in a villa near Palermo as 'blazing fire amongst the emerald boughs',[3] still resonates. In Richard Burton's *Book of the Thousand Nights and a Night* (1885), a garden of blood oranges in Cairo also provokes a vivid comparison:

> Red fruit that fill the hand, and shine with sheen of
>   fire . . .
> Like cheeks of women who their forms have decked
> for holiday in robes of gold brocade.[4]

A medieval Hispano-Arabic poem, 'The Orange' by Ibn Sara, thrillingly describes the fruit as 'tears reddened by the torments of love . . . frozen; but if they melted, they would be wine'.[5]

An old Spanish song or *copla* is almost haiku-like in its precise, sharp image:

> A branch of orange blossom:
> What a little thing it is,
> But how many oranges it gives.

De hortis Hesperidum by Giovanni Pontano (1426–1503) is a didactic poem inspired by the retired statesman's nostalgic recollection of the orange trees of his garden near Naples.[6] Pontanus was also the first to identify the citrus tree as the one in the Garden of the Hesperides that bore the so-called Golden Apples.

A century later, Pierre de Ronsard in one of his poignant sonnets for Hélène wrote:

> See how your orange and your lemon garnished
> by your sweet touch, token of love, are prest
> against my lips and cherished in my breast . . .[7]

A publicity shot from the California Valencia Orange Show. The show was held in Anaheim from 1921 to 1931.

Giovanni Battista Ferrarius pushed the hyperbolic limits in his great seventeenth-century citrus encyclopaedia, *Hesperides, sive, De Malorum Aureorum Cultura* (1646): 'So I bestow upon this little rounded fruit the merited name of an ornament of the world, for in its golden dress it seems a decoration for the earth.'[8]

The image of the orange tree as both gift and promise was an idyllic metaphor; but it could be turned on its head, as a character cynically comments in Webster's *The Duchess of Malfi* (1623): 'The orange tree bears ripe and green fruit, and blossoms all together: and some of you give entertainment for pure love; but more, for more precious reward.'

Stendhal defined the true south as the place where orange trees grow in the ground; the Mexican-American poet Gary

Soto offers a snapshot of adolescent love when he unpeels an orange so bright against the winter sky 'Someone might have thought / I was making a fire in my hands'; but in *Much Ado About Nothing* Shakespeare could affect to see through appearances, having Claudio compare Hero to a rotten orange whose 'blush is guiltiness, not modesty'. Again in *Much Ado*, Beatrice cleverly refers to Claudio's bitterness as 'civil as an orange, and something of that jealous complexion' – 'civil' perhaps being an ingenious pun on Seville. Was he, indeed, orange with jealousy?

Goethe invokes the haunting beauty of citrus trees when he asks, 'Do you know the land where the lemons bloom, / Oranges glow gold in leafy gloom . . .'. And he thinly disguises the potent imagery in 'To His Coy One':

Oh Orange,
Thou ripe and juicy Orange,
Thou sweet and luscious Orange,
I shake the tree, I shake it,
Oh fall into my lap!

More amusingly, in *Cranford* (1851–3), Elizabeth Gaskell has a delightful passage about how Miss Jenkyns and Miss Matty would eat their oranges:

Miss Jenkyns did not like to cut the fruit; for, as she observed, the juice all ran out nobody knew where; sucking (only I think she used a more recondite word) was in fact the only way of enjoying oranges; but then there was the unpleasant association with a ceremony frequently gone through by little babies; and so, after dessert, in orange season, Miss Jenkyns and Miss Matty used to rise up, possess themselves each of an orange in silence, and withdraw to the privacy of their own rooms, to indulge in sucking oranges.

Echoes appear in Iris Murdoch's *The Sea, The Sea* (1978) when she too describes how oranges should only be consumed in solitude. In *The Rituals of Dinner*, Margaret Visser quotes a Victorian manners books which sternly advises aspirational dinner guests to 'Never embark on an orange' at formal meals.[9]

The Orangery (1978), a collection of poems by Gilbert Sorrentino, is a self-contained literary tribute to the orange. Bound in orange, with orange endpapers and a picture of a branch on every page, the poems contain allusions to oranges in every sense. Even in the one sonnet that fails to mention the word, he wittily writes at the end, 'I forgot orange. There.'[10]

The orange transcends its nature in Pablo Neruda's 'Ode to the Orange' which begins, 'Just like you, / in your image, / orange, / the word was made: / the sun round, surrounded / by fiery rinds', then captures a sense of political unity: 'We are spokes of a single wheel divided like golden ingots'.[11]

In 'Other People's Glasshouses', English poet Ruth Pitter gently satirizes a visit to an English ducal garden,

But look where Orange-trees in fruit and bud
Bless our cold eyes, and stir nostalgic blood
To pine, as ever, for their odorous groves,
Their fireflies, and their Mediterranean loves![12]

The tree can also represents pain and grief, as in Lorca's 'Song of the Dead Orange Tree': 'Woodcutter. / Cut down my shadow. / Deliver me from the torment / of bearing no fruit.'[13] And the gentle domesticity of 'Sunday Morning' by Wallace Stevens (1879–1955) – 'Complacencies of the peignoir, and late / Coffee and oranges in a sunny chair' – soon gives way to a much deeper meditation on the nature of death and divinity.[14]

With heartbreaking lyricism W. B. Yeats reprises the Greek mythology of the Hesperides in 'The Song of Wandering Aengus':

> I will find out where she has gone,
> And kiss her lips and take her hands.
> And pluck till time and times are done
> The silver apples of the moon,
> The golden apples of the sun.[15]

The last, haunting line, a mirror of the fire in the writer's mind, also inspired a 1953 book of Ray Bradbury stories of that name, and interpretations by singers Donovan, Richie Havens and Judy Collins in the 1970s.

The 1950s Cockney slang term for homosexuals, 'As queer as a clockwork orange', caught the imagination of Anthony Burgess, who took it for the title of his novel of 1962. Jeanette Winterson used oranges in the title of her complex coming-of-age novel *Oranges Are Not the Only Fruit* (1985) to represent a whole set of rejected values.

The personal also becomes political in 'Orange Blossoms: A Palestinian Song' by Hasan al-Buhairi, a poem for a lost homeland. More often, though, the orange represents a gift of love, of life and future hope, as expressed by George Wallace in the poem 'Garden of the Nuns': 'Take this orange, Juanita. It holds the sun.'[16]

Another contemporary poet, Ronald Wallace, starts his celebratory poem 'Oranges' with an equally arresting sensory perception: 'This morning I eat an orange. / It is sour and juicy. My mouth / will tingle all day.'[17]

A play, *Blue/Orange* by Joe Penhall, was staged in London in 2000, and featured a bowl of oranges in a white stage set that in turn referenced the 1964 film *Tintin et les oranges bleues*.

Poster for Stanley Kubrick's film of *A Clockwork Orange* (1971).

Around the same time Mexican artist Gabriel Orozco persuaded the residents near MOMA in New York to place oranges on their windowsills to create an abstract pattern of dots in an intriguing art happening that 'made the everyday strange'.

Few children in the English-speaking world grow up without learning the 'Oranges and Lemons' nursery rhyme, a

Walter Crane (1845–1915), *Oranges and Lemons*. Crane was an English artist, part of the Arts and Crafts movement, who was an innovative children's book illustrator.

reminder of the time when the church bells of St Clements, Eastcheap rang when a cargo of citrus fruit from the Mediterranean arrived at the Thames wharf nearby. Recently, it was also the inspiration for British composer Benjamin Till's musical work that features every bell in every church mentioned in the longer version of the rhyme. 'The Love for Three Oranges' or, alternatively, 'The Three Citrons' refers to an Italian fairytale that was the basis for both a *commedia dell'arte* scenario and the Prokofiev opera.

To my mind, one of the most powerful comments on the fruit is a highly charged poem, 'Recipe for s&m Marmalade', by Judith Pacht.[18] It contains food, sex and violence. Plus blood oranges, the most ravishing citrus of all.

8
Art, Design and Culture

In a shop window on the King's Road, London, I spied a pair of men's underpants. They were printed with garish oranges and, at a strategic junction, bore the logo 'The Original Love Juice'.

The slogan is crude, but the sentiment has the endorsement of history. The Golden Apples of the Hesperides, now presumed to be either quince or, more likely, citrons, were a symbol of love in Greek tradition. The goddesses were the guardians of the gift given by Gaia to celebrate the bridal night of Zeus and Hera, whose union was heralded by a heavenly glow of sunset. It is thus possible to speculate that the European custom of giving oranges and tangerines at Christmas, so perfect to cushion the toe of a stocking, derives from the Demeter and Persephone story as a ritual of renewal and fertility.

Oranges are no longer the prerogative of gods and kings, but their cultivation has often been bound up with the magical and the divine as a result of the mysterious ability of the tree to simultaneously bear white flowers and golden fruit.

In Flemish legend, a young prince goes in search of a bride hidden within a magic orange in a land of sunshine and

Sir Edward Coley Burne-Jones, *The Garden of the Hesperides*, 1882, tempera and gilt on gesso on panel.

dark green groves.[1] *The Bee and the Orange* is a seventeenth-century French fairytale for adults, full of violence and thinly disguised social comment, in which the hero prince becomes a tree with whom the bee (really a princess) is in love. Wagner even gave the tree of golden apples its own leitmotif in *Das Rheingold* (1869).

The colour of the fruit linked them to the properties of blood and the life force, 'Live long, golden days amid the fruits of gold which prolong life', wrote Giovanni Battista Ferrarius in 1646. His prose-poem *Hesperides* is like a love letter:

> For this blossom, redolent of the whole springtime, puts life into one. Its little waxy cheek, breaking into spring laughter rejoices one. And the fact that it mingles useful-ness with its beauty is most satisfying.[2]

On the other hand, citrus has also played a part in vari-ous customs surrounding illness and death. The thirteenth-century count Henry of Sayn, for example, is portrayed on his tomb as holding a citrus fruit to symbolize the hope of resurrection and eternal life.

Santa Claus picking oranges in Sarasota, Florida, 1965.

At the Convent of S. Sabine in Rome, there is a sour orange tree (re-propagated in 1939) supposedly planted by St Dominic in the thirteenth century: it once was a charming custom for the nuns to pick and dry the fruit when small, and fashion them into rosaries to present to popes and cardinals.

Religious belief, however, can shade into superstition. Orange trees are no exception, especially when it comes to women. In some societies, women were held to have a malign influence should they go near one. Seville-born Ibn al-Awam wrote a comprehensive compendium on agriculture at the end of the twelfth century, although some of his inclusions may strike us as strange today. He stated, for example, that

> Women should not be allowed to come near citrus trees unless in a state of absolute purity and unimpaired health; if touched by a woman at the time of her period, it will wither and drop its leaves and part of its fruit.

In addition, he says, 'If a woman eat of an orange, or of a citron, or of a lemon, it will banish all evil thoughts from her mind.'[3] What a marketing slogan!

Oranges have also been a sign of wealth and exclusivity, a signifier of power suitable to present to high-ranking personages. In Venice on Ascension Day, it was once the custom for the Doge to offer a banquet to the local fishermen; in return, they would present him with oranges, muscat wine and gilded straw hats.

The trio of tributes recurs in the city's history in the Festa delle Marie, a celebration that commemorates the rescue of a dozen young girls from pirate clutches. Chateaubriand, recording a visit to the Lido in 1833, looked forward to a suitably lavish occasion. In the event, he was sorely disappointed, finding instead 'clumsy Austrian soldiers, in smocks and heavy boots, waltzing together, pipe to pipe, moustache to moustache: seized with horror, I threw myself into my gondola and returned to Venice'.[4]

By the eighteenth century, oranges and orange-flower water were perhaps the sun-dried tomatoes of their day, sought after by dedicated followers of fashion. Eliza Haywood, in an essay on 'Effeminacy in the Army Censured' (1745), was caustic about the bitter complaints made by London gentlemen at the wartime disruption of desired commodities:

> One who can endure no clothes that are not of the French cut, he is made a monster by a dunce of an English tailor; another is poisoned with ill scents, and dies for some fresh oranges and bergamot. A third says, pax on the Spanish War, and those that forced our late minister into it; there is not a bit of right vermillion paste now to be had![5]

She also quotes a bill from an army officer for, among other things, a night mask to take away freckles, a silver comb for the eyebrows and six bottles of orange-flower water.

Given the radiant glow of citrus fruit, it is easy to see their relevance to a festival that celebrates the end of winter. To this day, the Belgian town of Binche, before Ash Wednesday, holds a procession in which costumed *Gilles* (fanciful impersonations of Incas) offer oranges to the crowds from wicker baskets.

In fifteenth- and sixteenth-century Germany, towns would stage an annual archery festival. Tolkowsky says that at Breslau these festivals were known as *Pomeranzenschiessen* (orange-shooting). Winners would get a pewter platter with an orange, a beaker of wine and a wreath of roses (the loser had to make do with white cheese and a wreath of nettles on a wooden board). He also puts forward a fair case for William Tell's apple conceivably being an orange.[6]

The understandable enjoyment of giving, tossing and then throwing oranges became so popular among young people that the moralists of the day felt compelled to protest. In 1554, the Lutheran reformer Johannes Matthesius criticized the 'modern German girl' as a damsel who must needs drive about for pleasure, and have her own pocket-money; who writes love letters, does not shrink from throwing oranges down from her balcony, or from spending half her nights standing by the window.[7]

Another opportunity to hurl fruit, but with even greater vigour, is the Ivrea Carnival, north of Turin. Once a year the town has a few days of glory in which they stage an allegoric representation of an ancient insurrection against a local tyrant. It's a juicy orange battle in which the fruit represents arrows and stones, and leaves the streets carpeted with slippery, crushed oranges. Originally beans were thrown, then apples, but in the nineteenth century, oranges came to represent the decapitated head of the Duke, with the pulp and juice as his blood.

The link between oranges and festivities does not surprise. If any fruit lends itself to celebration, it surely must be the vivid hues and juicy elixir of the senior scion of the citrus family. The spectacular Fête du Citron in Menton boasts ever more grandiose forms and floats fabricated from both oranges and lemons; in Plaquemines, Louisiana, the Orange Festival includes pie-eating, orange-peeling and orange-rolling contests; there are cakes, biscuits, preserves and ice cream each year to celebrate the magnificent tarocco blood orange of Francofonte, Sicily; at the Lakeport Sour Orange Festival, Florida, the crowds enjoy sour orange pies and orange barbecue sauce; while another bitter orange festival in Bar-sur-Loup, Provence celebrates the local *bigarade* with a competition for the best orange wine producer. There are festivals in Tahiti, Cyprus, Mallorca, Tunisia and Puerto Rico; at the Festival de la Canción de la Naranja, Villa Alegre, Chile, the prize is a silver orange; one of the most popular events at the National

Orange Show Festival in Riverside, California is a piglet race (one rather hopes the losers avoid a medieval-style orange in the mouth fate); movingly, at the Bingara Orange Festival, Australia, local children pick the fruit in a tribute to the fallen of the two world wars in whose name the trees were planted; and, in Banyuls, France, along with the tarts, juice, jam and pies, there are inductions into the gloriously named Confrérie des Oranges Stressées.

The painting chosen by the Germanisches Nationalmuseum in Nuremberg to represent their 2011 exhibition on citrus fruit in art and culture was *The Orange Seller*, by Pierre-Nicolas Sicot-Legrand de Sérant, a late eighteenth-century allegory of the senses that is all ripe fruit, bare bosoms and zesty enticement.

The symbolism may be a little heavy-handed, but the work exudes beauty and exoticism, as well as fertility and purity simultaneously. The theme was not new. A few centuries earlier, Botticelli had depicted Venus surfing modestly on a scallop shell to a shore lined with orange trees.

In the history of art, orange trees are not simply beautiful, but take on deeper layers of meaning. They appear increasingly in the religious paintings of the Italian Renaissance as the backdrops become more lifelike and natural. Never having travelled to the Holy Land, the artists of the day set their Annunciations and Resurrections in Italian-style settings, turning the Tuscan landscape into a Palestinian one by the addition of citrus trees.

They are present in thousands of pictures illustrating every scene in the Gospel stories: indoors in moveable tubs, planted behind a building, forming a hedge, as a suspended backdrop or heavy with ripe fruit in the garden of Paradise. Duccio painted them in the Garden of Gethsemane; Fra

Angelico depicted Jesus resting under an orange tree; in Sano di Pietro's *Flight into Egypt* (1450–55), the protagonists pass by the orange tree of legend. As John McPhee pithily noted, 'It was almost unthinkable for a great master to do a "Flight into Egypt" without lining the route with orange trees.'[8] Citrus also plays its part in many a Last Supper: restoration work on Leonardo's famous *Last Supper* revealed eel and oranges on the table, a popular fish-and-fruit combo of the time.

The orange tree, because of its ability to simultaneously flower and fruit, also became a symbol of the Madonna. Her twin role as virgin and mother is depicted in paintings such as Ferrari's *Madonna degli Aranci* (1529–30), *The Holy Family* (*c.* 1512–13) by Joos van Cleve and the *Madonna of the Orange Tree* (*c.* 1495) by Cima da Conegliano.

In the great wave of still-life painting that spread across seventeenth-century Spain and the Netherlands, the intense depiction of the fruit reflected religious fervour, monetary value and natural beauty. In Spain, Francisco de Zurbarán painted them with dramatic light and shade, Luis Meléndez with studied geometric structure and lifelike precision, and for Bartolomé Esteban Murillo the fruit was a reflection of street life.

Market scenes of perfect fruit in northern Europe capture the sense of a new world order, prosperity and the triumph of trade. Decay is rarely seen in Dutch still-life; the tone is well-mannered and aspirational, suitable for the wealthy bourgeois patrons. In Jan van Eyck's *The Arnolfini Portrait* (1434) you can just about spot the oranges by the window, but they were deliberately included to show that the subject was a man of wealth and substance.

The peel spiral, as previously noted, might bring to mind the contemporary art of the mixologist, but it had other

Cima da
Conegliano,
*Madonna of
the Orange Tree,*
c. 1495, tempera
and oil on panel.

connotations. One interpretation is as a metaphor for the
journey of life, during which the outer material skin is gradually abandoned to reach the flesh, the spiritual essence.

Citrus was a status symbol, an object of conspicuous consumption either imported at considerable expense or pampered
in costly hothouses. Rubens's *The Walk in the Garden* (1630)
proudly displays the painter and his wife's ownership of four
young trees in pots around a tulip garden.

Lineage from the Dutch ruling dynasty of Orange-Nassau
was sometimes conveyed by a small tree. Other paintings were
even more oblique: in Jan Steen's *Prince's Day* (*c.* 1665), an

orange is strategically placed on the floor as a reference to the country's divided support for young Prince William III.

Botanical and artistic interest went hand in hand. Bartolomeo Bimbi's citrus paintings for the Medici were also a pictorial inventory. Vincenzo Leonardi made the innovative preparatory drawings for Ferrarius's *Hesperides*. A little later, in the first volume of the *Nuremberg Hesperides*, the beautifully illustrated fruits were pictured against a backdrop of Bavarian mansions; in the second, the villas of the Veneto; and in the recently discovered third volume, homes of the Bolognese nobility. It was another huge step forward in establishing botanical documentation as both a scientific discipline and a more refined art form.

Oranges have been painted to invoke expressions or moods, depict sensuality, for social comment or decoration, for their mythological or cultural associations and more, but of all the modern masters it was Matisse for whom they were more than just food or symbols. They were simply orbs of intense colour and joy. Simply themselves. According to the art critic Adrian Searle, 'He sent Picasso a box of

Francisco de Zurbarán, *Still-life with Lemons, Oranges and a Rose*, 1633, oil on canvas.

oranges once a year. Picasso never ate them, but had them on display – as Matisse's oranges, only to be looked at.'[9]

Citrus was also an important motif in other decorative forms: from the beginning of the Renaissance they adorned the festive table, reproduced in ceramic, porcelain and glass. The seventeenth-century German cities of Augsburg and Nuremberg were famous for elaborate silver fruit stands sculpted into entire garden scenes. Citrus was also found in stained glass windows, frescos, sculpture and more. In England, once citrus cultivation became a fashionable pastime of the nobility, the theme also played a part in lacework, embroidery and tapestry.

The tree has inspired some exquisite *objets*: Marie de' Medici is said to have owned an intricate jewel casket of gold and Limoges enamel with a large silver orange tree for a handle.[10] In 1911, Fabergé made an Easter egg for the Russian Royal Family in the shape of a miniature bay tree, albeit adorned with orange blossom and fruit, wrought from gold

Luis Meléndez, *Still-life with Oranges and Walnuts*, 1772, oil on canvas.

Jan van Eyck, *The Arnolfini Portrait*, 1434, oil on oak panel. Only the wealthy could afford either to cultivate or buy oranges in the 15th-century Netherlands.

and precious stones with a pop-up singing bird. Nearly 100 years later, the Hotel du Pont in Wilmington, Delaware, re-created it from sugar, chocolate, gold leaf and silver dust.

The fruit, too, has influenced modern commercial art and graphics, or rather the influence has been two-way. Californian and Floridian crate labels in the early twentieth century show a vivid creativity and eye-catching imagery, but they are also wonderful pieces of Americana.

In 1953, Bernard Villemot launched the fizzy orange drink Orangina's first advertising campaign poster featuring a para-sol shaped like an orange peel on a strong blue background. His design was bold, vivid and witty – a stylish telegram with a clear message.

The absorbing Museu de la Taronja near Valencia in Spain has a collection of more than 5,000 orange-box labels

Paul Cézanne, *Still-life with Apples and Oranges*, c. 1899, oil on canvas. Part of a series of still-lifes, the painting shows Cézanne's interest in shapes and forms, as well as minute variations in colour and tone.

plus hundreds of printed tissue-wrappers and posters. The museum also sponsored a contemporary orange-themed photographic contest for a number of years.

The world is full of oranges, there for our delectation, pleasure – and good health.

9
Health and Cookery

Poor Mary McCarthy in her Catholic girlhood was doomed to endure morning orange juice with castor oil 'brought . . . on the slightest pretext of "paleness".'[1]

The role of citrus in promoting good health, as both prophylactic and cure, has long been recognized if not always understood. The juice and peel were used as antidotes for poison (reassuring in a banquet); a twelfth-century Muslim writer prescribed powdered peel for colic and tapeworms; Dr Johnson was a staunch believer in the efficacy of dried and powered peel to cure indigestion when taken in a glass of hot, red port; and the *Tacuinum Sanitatis*, a vividly illustrated medieval Italian handbook on health and well-being based on an Arabic treatise, recommended the candied skin of ripe fruit as good for the stomach, although difficult to digest unless accompanied by the best wine.[2]

During the Renaissance, Italian physicians decided the scent of oranges would prevent the plague. Marsilio Ficino, a fifteenth-century Florentine scholar, suggested carrying 'odoriferous' citrus fruit and apples, and Domenico Romoli wrote in 1570 that 'to smell lemons, citrons or oranges in times of plague is a healthy thing'.[3] For much the same reason Cardinal Wolsey carried a Seville orange pomander, the hollowed-out flesh replaced with a sponge soaked in vinegar.[4] By Elizabethan and Jacobean times, the pomander had become an elaborate piece of jewellery, crafted from precious metals and gems.

Scurvy is caused by a lack of vitamin C, and it is believed that both Arab and Portuguese navigators had some knowledge of the connection. The latter planted citrus trees along their new trade routes – Madeira, the Azores, West Africa and St Helena – but by the eighteenth century the wisdom about their antiscorbutic properties seems to have largely vanished, with disastrous consequences for the British navy in particular. It took until 1747 for a Scottish physician to perform an experiment – perhaps the first clinical trial in history – to test a citrus fruit cure.

In search of a remedy for chronic indigestion, Robespierre was devoted to oranges, practically insatiable. He would have 'pyramids' placed on the table and ate them with 'extraordinary avidity'. According to his revolutionary contemporary Louis Fréron,

> No one ventured to touch the sacred fruit in his presence. No doubt the acidity acted on his bilious humours, and favoured their circulation. It was always easy to detect the place at table which he had occupied, by the piles of orange-peel which covered the plate. It was remarked, that as he ate them his severity of countenance relaxed.[5]

It is tempting to infer a connection between terror and citrus: Idi Amin lived his final years as a fruitarian, and bore the nickname 'Dr Jaffa' because of his love of oranges.

Nowadays, orange juice and health go together like Swanee and Dixie or Bill and Hillary. It is in part due to the genius of its marketing history that we automatically associate

Oranges and freshly squeezed juice. Freshly squeezed juice is the next best thing to consuming the fruit itself.

orange juice with all the things that are good for us, especially vitamin c.

As Pierre Laszlo says, every citrus fruit 'contains a most impressive pharmacopoeia', each one a miniature treasure trove of beneficial chemicals.[6] Oranges are indeed high in vitamin C, although blackcurrants and kiwi fruit are much higher. Organic oranges have been shown to contain up to 30 per cent more vitamin C than those grown conventionally, even when the latter are much larger.[7] Blood oranges, too, have significantly higher amounts of vitamin C and antioxidants than regular sweet oranges,[8] although the latter fade quickly once the orange is squeezed and pasteurized.

Juice, however, is only part of the whole fruit and might not be the best way to get the optimum health benefits in terms of vitamins and fibre. If your diet is already high in sugar, like most people's in the Western world, orange juice may be of less benefit than you imagine. Furthermore, the Harvard School of Public Health has pointed out that even if 100 per cent fruit juice has some vitamins, 'ounce for ounce [processed juice] contains as much sugar and calories as soda pop'.[9]

Fruit is meant to be eaten whole, and oranges provide more nutrition, including fibre, than juice. The Harvard School suggests that while a small glass (4 oz) of 100 per cent juice may be an enjoyable way to start the day, after that juice is just another high-calorie way to get water, while the American Academy of Pediatrics (AAP) advises that children under the age of six should drink just one cup a day of 100 per cent fruit juice, as too much juice in their diet may contribute to poor nutritional problems, obesity and tooth decay. Even older children should have a limit on their juice intake.[10] The message is clear. Juice you squeeze yourself is healthier than any in a carton or bottle that has gone through an industrial process. Better still, eat the orange.

The Arabs ate citrus fruit raw and sweetened, preserved them whole in sugar or candied the peel, but unlike the lemon, oranges do not take well to pickling. The first use of citrus in the West, however, was for either simple seasoning or ornamental purposes. Ugo Falcando, a twelfth-century Sicilian, wrote about 'oranges which although full of acid juice, are more apt to please the eye in account of their beauty than to be put to any other use'.[11]

Before the Crusades, tart fruit and leaves, vinegar and verjuice were used as souring or de-greasing agents in Northern Europe. It was probably in the Holy Land that warriors, pilgrims and merchants learnt how citrus could enhance the salted staples of the colder regions. Their scent likely also helped relieve the stuffy and unsanitary atmosphere of many a medieval castle. The use of oranges for seasoning may have started later than that of lemons, but the natural affinity with fish in particular was quickly embraced.

Renaissance cooks used the fruit, peel and juice in the same ostentatious way they did all precious commodities. A dinner given by the abbé de Lagny for the bishop of Paris in the fourteenth century included several kinds of roast fish served with sour oranges and powdered sugar. In Gillian Riley's view, they played the same role in Renaissance art as they did in gastronomy, adding 'grace notes of cheerfulness and sparkle to the rich complexities of a composition, be it banquet or altarpiece'.[12]

There are references to fried oranges with leveret pies at a feast given by the Comté de Foix in 1457, and in 1546 in Venice, a plate of stuffed oranges accompanied herring fillets with orange juice.[13] Platina, in *De honesta voluptate et valetudine* (1474), includes oranges from Naples in a list of top regional specialities of the day.[14] The first written recipe for bitter oranges in German dates from 1485, when they are described as 'small, sour apples from Italy' and the author suggests cooking them with wine and cinnamon to make a sauce for poultry and game.[15] The combination of partridge and orange became such a culinary cliché that a political pamphlet of 1594 made the pithy charge, 'A Spaniard without a Jesuit is like a partridge without an orange.'[16]

The famous Renaissance chef Bartolomeo Scappi, in his monumental *Opera* (1570), recommends various ways of cooking fish, including fried in oil and served hot with a bitter orange sauce.[17] He also proposes an interesting relish of bitter oranges and quince.

By the start of the sixteenth century, citrus was also firmly established as part of the English culinary repertoire. Fish day feasts would include baked oranges and orange fritters, and in 1522 Henry Willoughby, a Midlands landowner, spent eight pence on 100 oranges during a stay in London.[18] A festive Elizabethan way of cooking pike was to boil it in wine with oranges, dates and spices: according to C. Anne Wilson: 'It was neatly dissected first, and reassembled for serving, when its head was placed upright with an orange in its mouth.'[19]

In 1529, a dinner given by Ercole d'Este in Ferrara featured fried trout with lemon, roast pheasants with 'split' oranges, and mixed salad with slices of citron. The same year, Ippolito d'Este, archbishop of Milan (whose chef was the famous Cristoforo da Messisbugo), more than matched this with a banquet of several hundred dishes and sixteen courses, not counting sweets and fruit. It included salad of herbs and citron cut into the initials of guests' names and their coats of arms; caviar fried with oranges covered with sugar and cinnamon; fried sardines with oranges; a thousand oysters with oranges and pepper; a salad of lobster tails and citrons; sturgeon in orange jelly; sparrows fried with oranges; orange fritters with sugar and cinnamon . . . on, and on, into citrus infinity.[20]

On the more modest domestic front, citrus juice was increasingly used with poultry and veal as well as fish, and the whole fruit enhanced meat stews. Sugar or honey was added to meat and fish dishes to moderate the bitterness, and slices of fruit made colourful garnishes. According to C. Anne Wilson, bitter orange juice was particularly favoured by fifteenth-century pregnant women.[21] She also notes how baked oranges were served for the enthronement feast of Archbishop Warham in 1505 – but only the nobility enjoyed orange fritters the next day.

Curiously, German miners in the Lake District in the 1560s were provided with oranges and artichokes from London,[22] although we can only speculate on whether they were more sophisticated in their tastes than the locals, or whether the use of oranges had by then percolated down the social scale.

By 1604, Lady Elinor Fettiplace was compiling elegant receipts for dishes such as roast mutton with Seville orange juice, spices and claret wine gravy. Interestingly, the Seville orange season in the seventeenth century seems to have enviably run from November to April, and the fruit could be eaten year-round, 'dried, crystallised, candied, stuffed, bottled and floating in syrup or jelly, or boiled to a thick sweet paste called "marmalade"'.[23]

A few years later, in his book *Delights for Ladies* (1609), Sir Hugh Plat suggests a show-stopping way for preserving oranges 'after the Portugall fashion'. The lustrous whole poached fruit, stuffed with puréed flesh and peel, can be presented intact and 'cut like a hard egg'. He also includes a recipe for candied orange peel in sugar and rosewater. Such candied or preserved 'orangeadoes' were a modish snack of the time, nibbled at the theatre or proffered in fashionable drawing rooms.

In France, citrus replaced verjuice in sauces, and the peels too were candied for sweetmeats. As China oranges made their mark, they were deemed too sweet to accompany savoury foods, and both the fruit and scented orange-flower water were used in puddings, creamy concoctions, cakes and biscuits. Barbara Ketcham Wheaton notes a sixteenth-century recipe in *Le Viandier*, a recipe collection dating in its earliest incarnation to the fourteenth century, that heralded a new direction in French cooking: a foamy mix of egg yolks, sugar, cinnamon, orange juice and rosewater, heavy with cinnamon and 'extraordinarily sweet'.[24] She also points to La Varenne's great cookbook, *Le Cuisinier françois* (1651), a founding text of modern French cuisine that breaks decisively with the Middle Ages, citing a recipe for mutton daube with herbs and orange peel 'but very little for fear of bitterness': as she says, the age of cinnamon and pepper was over and the new cookery was to be characterized by moderation and subtlety but never blandness.[25]

Nicolas de Bonnefons in *Les Délices de la campagne* (1662) recommended the use of oranges with roasted chestnuts: 'You shall pour orange juice over them, this being their true sauce, and powder them with sugar.' He also gave a useful kitchen tip: 'To obtain a lot of juice from an orange, beat it and warm it a short while over the fire.'[26]

Paintings by artists such as Luis Meléndez also tell a story, as Gillian Riley has noted. In the case of *Still Life with Oranges and Walnuts* (1772), it was that of the household's winter store-cupboard, including the 'joyful orbs of the first oranges of the season'.[27]

A verse on street cries by Jonathan Swift in early eighteenth-century London gives a clue to oranges' kitchen use at the time:

Come, buy my fine oranges, sauce for your veal,
And charming, when squeezed in a pot of brown ale:

Jean-Siméon Chardin, *Un Canard col-vert attaché a la muraille et une brigarade*, *c.* 1730.

Well roasted, with sugar and wine in a cup,
They'll make a sweet Bishop [punch] when gentlefolk sup.

Some cultures appreciate the taste of the rind. In Athol
Fugard's play *The Island* (1973), an African eats an orange
whole. Margaret Visser noted that at the London opening
night the audience was blasé about the nude scenes, but

gasped in horror at the sight of someone biting into an unpeeled orange.[28]

The juice of the sour orange is often used as a marinade in Latin America; in Mexico, sour oranges are cut in half, salted and coated with a paste of hot chilli peppers; and Seville oranges make a distinctive appearance in Cadiz fish soup.

The bitter orange pairs well with duck and other game. As the French philosopher and writer Jean-François Revel points out, the alliance of sweet and salt, of meat and fruit was normal practice from the Middle Ages until the seventeenth century.[29] Nonetheless, the earliest written French recipes for combining duck and oranges seem to date only to the nineteenth century when Louis Eustache Ude described ducklings *à la bigarade* as 'a dish for an epicure of the daintiest palate'.[30] In modern dinner party circles, duck with orange reached its zenith in the 1960s and '70s, when it also held pole position in restaurant menus alongside crêpes Suzette.

Cooking with oranges is now mainstream, but the fruit continues to inspire. I have found one Spanish chef in Aranjuez who seasons grouper with a mix of Maldon salt and dehydrated orange skin, and in 2011 Heston Blumenthal took London by storm when he disguised a ball of chicken liver pâté in opaque aspic to look like a citrus fruit with glistening peel and shiny leaves. Arguably, it has become the signature dish of the decade, akin to an Ancient Roman jest, a medieval subtlety, a Renaissance flourish, or a Baroque extravagance. It is the triumph of the orange.

10

Marmalade

The eighteenth-century Scottish author James Boswell wrote of one blissful February morning: 'Breakfast, sunshine, marmalade.' The simple sentiment is timeless.

Marmalade wakes up the matutinal tastebuds, much as a cold shower does the body. Beloved of the British breakfast table, marmalade inspires nostalgia, strong opinions and deep loyalties.

The origins of marmalade lie in an ancient technique of preserving peel or the whole fruit in syrup. Such *succades* were exported to Northern Europe in medieval times, but the first wooden boxes of Portuguese *marmelada* only arrived in Britain at the end of the fifteenth century: made with quinces (*marmelo*), the costly conserve was firm enough to cut with a knife. In due course, English housewives learnt to make both syrups and pastes from citrus and home-grown quinces.[1]

By the sixteenth century, citrus trees had spread throughout the West Indies. Friar Joseph de Acosta, a natural historian, wrote in 1590 that the 'conserve of oranges' there (probably made with a bittersweet orange) was the best he had tasted anywhere. The use of slivers of peel was introduced in the seventeenth century, and the eighteenth saw a new transparent 'jelly' with a little finely cut peel, but it was generally still dense and solid.

Marmalade as we know it is popularly believed to have been invented in Scotland when James Keiller bought a cargo of Sevilles that could not be moved from Dundee harbour because of fierce storms. Unable to sell the fruit, his wife made it into jam. The story, however, doesn't quite stand up: orange preserve was a known product by the time Keiller founded his firm in 1797 and the first printed recipe in English for pippin-free marmalade (the pippin pectin made it very firm) dates back to 1714.[2] However, it does seem true that Scottish cooks readily substituted Seville oranges for quinces, adjusted the proportion of water to give a softer consistency, promoted 'chip' marmalade and, significantly, served it at breakfast rather than after supper. Both the peel and the sugar, as C. Anne Wilson comments, were 'warming to the cold early morning stomach'.[3]

Citrus products display, Indian River, Florida, 1949.

The late nineteenth century was the golden age of marmalade. Commercial brands such as Robertson's Fine-cut Golden and Silver Shred, Frank Cooper's coarse-cut 'Oxford' and Chivers Olde English swept the market. Store-bought was no badge of shame but a mark of patriotic pride. According to Wilson, Wilkin of Tiptree was producing some 27 different marmalades by the turn of the century.[4]

The annual Dalemain Marmalade Awards and Festival in Cumbria is a fiercely contested competition and slightly eccentric celebration of all things marmalade. Curiously, domestic marmalade making is a culinary operation often performed by men – the cold weather equivalent of the barbecue, perhaps.

Marmalade ranges from single to multi-fruit, pale gold to mahogany, chunky and rind-thick to transparent and semiliquid with slivers of peel. It can be flavoured with whisky or rum and ginger or other spices. A marmalade-flavoured vodka has even been launched on the British market, and a marmalade cocktail features on the list at the popular Hawksmoor Spitalfields bar in London. Marmalade has been to the Antarctic and up Everest. James Bond would always breakfast on Frank Cooper's. In 1629, English playwright Philip Massinger wrote admiringly of a lady with marmalade lips, and 300 years later The Beatles sang of marmalade skies. Best of all, Paddington Bear has always ascribed his youthful looks to a never-ending love of marmalade sandwiches. I rest my case.

Recipes

Citrus Marinade

In the sixteenth century, one Italian traveller to the Molucca Islands wrote about the cannibals of a certain island who, as quoted in Tolkowsky's *Hesperides: A History of the Culture and Use of Citrus Fruits*, 'eat no other part of the human body but the heart; uncooked but seasoned with the juice of oranges and lemons'. I suggest this marinade be used for seafood or salmon instead.

250 ml (9 fl. oz) fresh orange juice
150 ml (5 fl. oz) fresh lemon juice
150 ml (5 fl. oz) fresh lime juice
100 ml (3 ½ fl. oz) olive oil
2–3 cloves of garlic, finely chopped
1 tablespoon grated orange zest
fresh coriander, chopped

Combine all the ingredients except the coriander and marinate the seafood in the mixture for 30 minutes before grilling or frying. Brush with the marinade a few times while it cooks. Sprinkle with the coriander before serving.

Serves 4

Broccoli with Orange Peel and Walnuts

A homage to Chinese citrus origins.

1 orange
1 tablespoon oil
25 g (1 oz) walnuts
200 g (7 oz) broccoli, cut into florets
1 tablespoon soy sauce
1 teaspoon red chilli pepper, finely chopped
1 teaspoon fresh root ginger, grated

Use a vegetable peeler to remove the orange peel in small strips (avoiding the pith). Juice the orange and set aside. Heat the oil in a nonstick pan or wok. Add the orange peel and nuts and fry very briefly for 1–2 minutes until the peel just turns golden at the edges. Add the ginger and chilli, then the broccoli. Sprinkle with the juice. Fry for a few minutes and add the soy sauce. Fry for a minute more, stir well and serve.

Serves 2–3

Scallops and Oranges à la Pepys

Samuel Pepys refers to a box of China oranges and two little barrels of scallops in his diary entry for 16 February 1660. It is unlikely that they would have been eaten or cooked together, but it is nonetheless a mild indulgence to imagine that he might have enjoyed this recipe.

4 tablespoons vegetable oil
8 diver-caught scallops seasoned with salt and pepper
2 cloves of garlic, finely chopped
120 ml (½ cup) freshly squeezed orange juice
½ teaspoon grated orange zest
1 tablespoon soy sauce

Heat 3 tablespoons of the oil in a large frying pan. Sauté the scallop briefly on both sides until just brown. Place on warm serving plate

Add the remaining oil and the garlic to the pan and stir until the aroma rises. Add the orange juice, zest and soy sauce. Stir a few minutes until the sauce boils and thickens, then pour over the scallops. Serve straight away.

Serves 4, as a starter

Sole Meunière à l'Orange

Auguste Escoffier lists an extraordinary 114 recipes for sole in *Le Guide Culinaire* (1903). The playwright Paul Schmidt, in his essay 'As If a Cookbook Had Anything to Do with Writing', described the delirious impact of the roll-call of names, colours, balloons, queens and courtesans thus: 'what is intended as a most precise kind of inventory becomes glittering caprice.'

I am not sure Escoffier's *sole meunière à l'orange* can really be described as a separate recipe from the ur-meunière method he gives, since the only difference is the addition of orange slices or segments as topping. But, I bow to the *maître*, and offer this slight update in respect.

2 sole or other flat fish, filleted
120 ml (½ cup) fresh orange juice
70 g (½ cup) plain (all-purpose) flour, seasoned with salt and
black and cayenne pepper
4 tablespoons unsalted butter (or clarified butter)
peeled orange slices or segments
coarsely chopped parsley

Dip the fish fillets in the orange juice, then in the flour. Over a high heat, add half the butter to a large frying pan until it melts but does not brown. Add the fillets and cook for a few minutes on each side. Place on heated plates and garnish with the orange slices and chopped parsley.

Now add the rest of the butter to the pan and heat rapidly until the butter foams and starts to turn nutty brown. Pour over the fish and serve at once.

Serves 2

Mexican Orange Chicken

Citrus went west, along with chicken – and the New World kitchen was never the same again.

6 chicken portions
2 tablespoons oil
1 onion, chopped
2 cloves of garlic, chopped
2 whole cloves
half a cinnamon stick
juice of 2 oranges
150 ml (⅔ cup) water
A few sprigs of thyme
2 bay leaves
sea salt and black pepper to taste

In a large frying pan, fry the chicken until golden. Remove and set aside while you fry the onion till soft. Add the garlic and fry until the aroma rises. Add the cloves and cinnamon, then return the chicken to the pan. Pour over the orange juice and water, and add the herbs. Season to taste.

Bring to the boil, reduce heat, cover and simmer until the chicken is cooked, about 35–40 minutes. Serve with white rice or add sliced parboiled potatoes to the chicken while it cooks.

Serves 6

Steak with Red Wine Citrus Sauce

This medieval recipe, based on one by the late food historian Maggie Black, originally used verjuice as an alternative to bitter orange, but you can substitute sweet orange and lemon juice.

4 beef or venison steaks
oil for cooking
1 tablespoon red wine vinegar
8 teaspoons red wine
4 tablespoons Seville orange juice (or 3 tablespoons sweet orange juice and 1 tablespoon lemon juice)
2 tablespoons water
1 tablespoon dark brown sugar
2 grindings of black pepper
1 teaspoon ground ginger
cinnamon
sea salt

Mix all the sauce ingredients except the cinnamon and salt in a small pan. Bring to the boil and take off the heat. Allow to infuse for five minutes. Taste the sauce and add more water or sugar if desired.

Nick the edges of the steaks and lightly grease them with oil. Heat a thick-based frying pan or griddle and sear the steaks on both sides, then reduce the heat and cook until done to your preference, turning as required. Sprinkle a few drops of the sauce over the steaks on each side as they cook.

Lightly dust the steaks with cinnamon and sea salt. Pour some sauce over each one, and, as we used to say in the fifteenth century, 'Serve it forth'.

Serves 4

Sicilian Pork Escalopes with Oranges

I am grateful for this recipe from Signora Serafina Giannalia of Palermo, who made an unplanned stay in a Sicilian fracture clinic unexpectedly entertaining.

This can also be made with chicken or veal.

6 pork escalopes coated in beaten egg and breadcrumbs
4 tablespoons olive oil
4–5 shallots
12 cherry tomatoes, halved
2 oranges – one juiced and the other cut into thin slices
dried oregano
salt and pepper

Chop the shallots and fry in oil until soft. Add the tomatoes. Push the vegetables to one side and add the escalopes. Fry until brown on each side. Add the orange juice to the pan, and arrange the orange slices on top of the escalopes. Sprinkle with a little oregano, salt and pepper. Cover and cook on a low heat for about ten minutes.

Serves 6

Spiced Caramel Oranges

An Italian classic with a modern twist.

6 oranges
225 g (8 oz) sugar
225 ml (1 cup) water
2 cinnamon sticks
2 star anise

Zest the oily outer orange rind and shred finely. Set aside.

Cut the remaining skin and white pith from the oranges and slice horizontally. Arrange in a dish.

Heat the sugar, half the water and spices and stir until the sugar dissolves. Leave to simmer, without stirring, until the sugar turns caramel. Remove the spices.

Hold the pan over the sink and carefully add the remaining water – be careful, it's likely to spit. Stir to remove any lumps.

Pour most of the caramel over the oranges. Simmer the zest in the remaining caramel for a few minutes and drizzle over the fruit.

Serves 4

Orange Omelette for Brazen Harlots and Ruffians

Johannes Bockenheim, fifteenth-century cook to Pope Martin v, was very precise about the demographics for this dish in his small volume *Registrum Coquine*: Take eggs and break them, with oranges, as many as you like; squeeze their juice and add to it the eggs with sugar; then take olive oil or fat, and heat it in the pan and add the eggs. *Et erit bonum.* Another egg and orange recipe was for 'pimps and lecherous women'.

The following recipe is an update of the above, courtesy of Odile Redon et al., authors of *The Medieval Kitchen: Recipes from France and Italy* (2000). (The sugar and the acidity of the juice prevents the eggs from completely setting, so this is more of a custardy cream dessert.) As they add, rather like a government health warning, 'This omelette can be safely tasted without running the risk of moral turpitude.'

2 oranges
2 lemons
6 eggs
2 tablespoons sugar
salt to taste
olive oil

Juice the oranges and lemons. Beat the eggs, add the juice, two tablespoons of sugar and salt to taste, and cook in olive oil. Serve warm.

Serves 2–3

Crêpes Suzette

There are two versions of the history of this classic dish. In the first, the young waiter and future chef Henri Charpentier claims to have accidentally ignited a pancake flavoured with cognac at Monte Carlo's Café de Paris in 1895. He was preparing the dessert for the Prince of Wales and his companion Princess Suzanne, and later described the happy discovery in his autobiography, *Life à la Henri* (1934), as a confection 'one taste of which, I really believe, would reform a cannibal into a civilised gentleman'. A competing claim contends that the dish was named in 1897 in honour of the Comédie Française actress Suzanne Reichenberg.

In one of the most iconic episodes of her television series, *The French Chef*, the inimitable Julia Child made crêpes bathed in an orange butter and liqueur sauce. There have been many variations over the years; this is based on one by the equally legendary Robert Carrier.

For the crêpes:
75 g plain flour (1 cup plus ¼ oz), sifted with a pinch of salt
2 large eggs, beaten
25 g (1 oz) unsalted butter, melted
200 ml (7 fl. oz) milk
vegetable oil or melted clarified butter

For the orange butter:
100 g (3½ oz) unsalted butter
25 g (1 oz) caster sugar
finely grated zest of 1 large orange

30 ml (1 fl. oz) Cointreau or Grand Marnier
75 ml (⅓ cup) orange juice

To flame:
1 tablespoon caster sugar
2 tablespoons Cointreau
2 tablespoons brandy

Place the flour in a mixing bowl and beat in the eggs and butter. Gradually stir in the milk until the batter is as thin as single cream. Add a little water if necessary. Strain the batter through a fine sieve and leave to stand for at least two hours.

Heat a small crêpe pan, remove from the heat and rub the bottom and sides with a piece of kitchen paper saturated with oil or clarified butter. Spoon about 2 tablespoons of batter into the pan, swirling the pan so that the batter covers the base thinly. Cook over a medium heat for about a minute, then run a palette knife around and under the crêpe to loosen it. Flip it over and cook for a further minute. (If you're hesitant to toss, try using a spatula.) Repeat until all the batter is used up, greasing the pan again if necessary. Stack the cooked crêpes on a plate as they are ready.

For the orange butter, melt the butter in a large frying pan, and add the other ingredients for the orange butter. Simmer for a few minutes. Keeping the heat low, place a crêpe in the pan of orange butter, and use a fork and spoon to fold it in half, then quarters. Push to the side of the pan and repeat with the remaining crêpes.

When they are all in the pan (and it does not matter if they overlap), sprinkle with caster sugar. Pour the Cointreau and brandy into a small pan and warm over a low heat. Stand well clear and use a long match to set the alcohol alight. Pour the flaming alcohol over the crêpes and serve immediately.

Serves 6

Tarte of Apples and Orenge Pilles

Pilles is the medieval word for peel, and this recipe is based on that given in *The Good Huswifes Handmaide for the Kitchin*, published in London at the end of the sixteenth century. I am grateful to Gretchen Miller for this modern redaction.

For the filling:
6 medium oranges (Valencia, blood or Sevilles, but not navels as the skins are too thick)
1 litre (1¾ pints) water
300 g (10½ oz) honey
14 small McIntosh or cooking apples
200 g (7 oz) sugar
1 teaspoon cinnamon
½ teaspoon ground ginger
2 tablespoons rosewater
1 tablespoon sugar

For the pastry:
350 g (12 oz) flour
3 egg yolks
120 g (4 oz) butter
6 tablespoons water
3 egg yolks

First, soak the oranges in water for 24 hours. When this is done, in a large saucepan, mix the honey with the water used to soak the oranges, add the oranges, bring to a boil, and simmer until the peel on the oranges feels soft. Place the oranges in a container and pour the syrup over them. Put a plate or other heavy object on top of the oranges to hold them under the syrup, adding a little water if there is not enough to completely cover the oranges. Cover the container and leave to soak for 24 hours.

When the oranges are ready, preheat the oven to 180°C (350°F), and mix the flour and egg yolks for the pastry. Put the butter and water in a small saucepan over a low heat until the butter is melted, then add to the flour and egg mixture. Knead until it becomes a dough ball. If extra water is needed, add 1 teaspoon. Divide in two and roll out each half into a circle about 23 cm (9 in) in diameter. Place one on a baking tray.

Slice the oranges and remove the seeds. If the syrup has not completely saturated the rinds, boil the slices in the syrup. Chop the oranges into small pieces or blend. Mix with half the sugar, cinnamon and ginger.

Now peel, core and quarter the apples, and mix with the remaining sugar and spices. Place a layer of apples on the bottom of the piecrust, covering with a layer of oranges. Repeat. Top with the other pastry round, crimp the edges and bake for 1 hour.

Ten minutes before the pie finishes baking, mix 2 tablespoons of rosewater and 1 tablespoon of sugar over a low heat until syrupy. Remove the pie from the oven, brush on the rosewater syrup and return to the oven until the hour is up. (Note: the original recipe suggests the rosewater syrup should be brushed onto the pastry lid with a feather.)

Rhubarb and Blood Orange Marmalade

A lovely variation on the theme.

> 2.5 kg (5½ lbs) rhubarb, cut into small pieces
> 2 kg (4½ lbs) granulated sugar
> 2 blood oranges

Layer the rhubarb and sugar and leave for twelve hours.

When the rhubarb is ready, gently boil the oranges whole until tender (about 1 hour). Quarter, remove the pips and slice finely. Place in a preserving pan with the rhubarb and sugar. Heat gently and stir until the sugar is dissolved. Bring to the boil and cook rapidly until the setting point is reached. Pour into sterilized pots, cover and seal as usual.

Orange Drinks

Orange Julius

A nostalgic American childhood favourite.

250 ml (9 fl. oz) fresh or reconstituted frozen orange juice
60 ml (2 fl. oz) milk
1 teaspoon vanilla extract
2 tablespoons sugar
1 scoop of vanilla ice cream
handful of ice cubes

Blend all the ingredients until smooth and serve in chilled glasses. If the mixture is too thick, add more juice or water; if too thin, add more ice or ice cream.

Cuban Rose

This first appeared in *The Old Waldorf-Astoria Bar Book* published in 1935, an excellent read on the origins of modern cocktails with intriguing stories of pre-Prohibition days.

For one cocktail:
⅓ orange juice
⅔ Bacardi (or other white rum)
dash of grenadine

Pour the ingredients into a cocktail shaker. Note that the order of adding ingredients is important. Shake well, and pour into a glass containing freshly shaved ice.

Mimosa

15 ml (1 tablespoon) triple sec
50 ml (2 fl. oz) fresh orange juice
100 ml (3 1/2 fl. oz) champagne
orange slice for garnish

Pour the ingredients into a champagne flute in the order given and garnish with the orange slice.

References

1 The History of Oranges

1 W. T. Swingle and P. C. Reece, 'The Botany of Citrus and Its Wild Relatives', chap. 3 of *The Citrus Industry* (Riverside, CA, 1967), vol. I.

2 University of Western Sydney press release, 'Scientists Claim Citrus Originated in Australasia' (1 October 2007), at http://phys.org, accessed 10 July 2012.

3 Samuel Tolkowsky, *Hesperides: A History of the Culture and Use of Citrus Fruits* (London, 1938), p. 4.

4 Joseph Needham, *Science and Civilisation in China* (Cambridge, 1986), VI/1, p. 363.

5 Frederick G. Gmitter and Xulan Hu, 'The Possible Role of Yunnan, China, in the Origin of Contemporary Citrus Species (rutaceae)', *Economic Botany*, XLIV/2 (1990), pp. 267–7.

6 Needham, *Science and Civilisation*, pp. 363–77.

7 Ibid.

8 Tolkowsky, *Hesperides*, p. 11. (The purple gauze is for straining.)

9 Ibid., pp. 101–18.

10 Alfred C. Andrews, 'Acclimatization of Citrus Fruits in the Mediterranean Region', *Agricultural History*, XXXV/1 (1961), pp. 35–46.

11 L. Ramón-Laca, 'The Introduction of Cultivated Citrus to Europe via Northern Africa and the Iberian Peninsula',

Economic Botany, LVII/4 (Winter, 2003).

12 Margaret Visser, *Much Depends on Dinner* (London, 1989), p. 265.

13 Barbara Santich, *The Original Mediterranean Cuisine* (Totnes, 1995), p. 27.

14 Ibid., p. 28.

15 E. G. Ravenstein, ed. and trans., *A Journal of the First Voyage of Vasco da Gama, 1497–1499* (London, 1898), p. 34.

16 Tolkowsky, *Hesperides*, pp. 236–8.

17 Herbert John Webber, 'History and Development of the Citrus Industry', chap. 1 of *The Citrus Industry,* vol. 1.

18 Ibid.

19 Tolkowsky, *Hesperides*, p. 247.

20 Ibid, p. 227.

21 Mark Morton, 'Hue and Eye', *Gastronomica*, XI/3 (Fall 2011).

22 Webber, 'History and Development of the Citrus Industry'.

23 John F. Mariani, *The Encyclopedia of American Food and Drink* (New York, 1999), p. 273.

24 Food Resource website, Oregon State University, http://food.oregonstate.edu.

25 Peter Hammond, *Food and Feast in Medieval England* (Stroud, 2005), p. 12.

26 Nancy Cox and Karin Dannehl, *Dictionary of Traded Goods and Commodities, 1550–1820* (Wolverhampton, 2007).

2 Cultivation

1 John McPhee, *Oranges* (London, 2000), p. 67.

2 Ibn Battuta, *Travels in Asia and Africa, 1325–1354*, at www.fordham.edu, accessed 10 July 2012.

3 Samuel Tolkowsky, *Hesperides: A History of the Culture and Use of Citrus Fruits* (London, 1938), p. 192.

4 Ibid., p. 193.

5 John Parkinson, *Paradisi in sole paradisus terrestris* [1629] (London, 1904), p. 584.

6 Tolkowsky, *Hesperides,* p. 203.

7 Waverley Root, *Food* (New York, 1980), p. 304.

8 Dominique Garrigues, *Jardins et Jardiniers de Versailles au Grand Siècle* (Seyssel, 2001), p. 145 (author's trans.).

3 Classification

1 D. J. Mabberley, 'A Classification for Edible Citrus', *Telopea* 7(2) (1997), pp. 167–72.

2 The Orange (*Citrus Sinensis*) Annotation Project, at http://citrus.hzau.edu.cn, accessed 9 July 2012.

3 Julia F. Morton, *Fruits of Warm Climates* (Miami, FL, 1987), pp. 130–33.

4 Some authorities contend that the myrtle leaf is a separate species.

5 Robert Willard Hodgson, 'Horticultural Varieties of Citrus', chap. 4 of *The Citrus Industry* (Riverside, CA, 1967), vol. I.

6 Samuel Tolkowsky, *Hesperides: A History of the Culture and Use of Citrus Fruits* (London, 1938), p. 158.

7 James Saunt, *Citrus Varieties of the World* (Norwich, 1990), p. 24.

8 'Solved: The Mystery of the Blood Orange', www.sciencecodex.com, 19 March 2012.

9 Martin et al., 'Retrotransposons Control Fruit-specific, Cold-dependent Accumulation of Anthocyanins in Blood Oranges', *The Plant Cell*, XXIV (2012).

10 Saunt, *Citrus Varieties*, p. 26.

4 Business and Trade

1 John Dickie, *Cosa Nostra: A History of the Sicilian Mafia* (London, 2007), p. 26.

2 J. Joseph, *Squeezing Children to Make Orange Juice, Tomatoes and Raspberries* (report by Made in the USA Foundation, 1999).

3 Sonja Salzburger, Council on Hemispheric Affairs, 'Made in Brazil: Confronting Child Labor' (16 November 2010),

at www.coha.org, accessed 10 July 2012.

4 Jo Southall, 'Juicy Dilemmas: Ethical Shopping Guide to Fruit Juice' (2010), at www.ethicalconsumer.org, accessed 10 July 2012.

5 Jane Daugherty, *Palm Beach Post* (December 2003).

6 Coalition of Immokalee Workers, at http://ciw-online.org, accessed 9 July 2012.

7 Gianluca Martelliano and Andrew Wasley, 'Coca Cola Responds to Orange Harvest "Exploitation" Controversy', *The Ecologist* (26 February 2012).

8 'Protecting a Citrus Tree from Cold' (2001), at http://ag.arizona.edu, accessed 9 July 2012.

9 Often referred to *Huanglongbing* or HLB.

10 Kevin Bouffard, 'Citrus Growers and Scientists Discuss Nutrition Research' (25 August 2011), at www.theledger.com, accessed 10 July 2012.

11 Evan D. G. Fraser and Andrew Rimas, *Empires of Food* (New York and London, 2010), p. 163.

12 Amanda Garris, 'Plant Pathologists Put the Squeeze on Citrus Disease' (17 January 2012), at http://phys.org, accessed 10 July 2012.

13 Rod Santa Ana, 'Spinach Genes May Stop Deadly Citrus Disease' (27 March 2012), at http://phys.org, accessed 9 July 2012.

14 Charles Johnson, 'A "Silver Bullet" for Citrus Greening?' (2 February 2012), at www.southeastfarmpress.com, accessed 10 July 2012; 'Scientists Release Natural Enemy of Asian Citrus Psyllid' (20 December 2011), at www.newsroom.ucr.edu, accessed 10 July 2012.

15 Organic citrus may be coated with non-synthetic wax to prolong storage after washing, and non-organic citrus with paraffin wax. Both should be scrubbed in warm, soapy water if the peel is to be used. If possible, buy fruit labelled wax-free. Citrus dye is also prohibited in certain U.S. states. Both conventional and organic growers may choose to use ethylene gas to give the fruit a better colour.

5 Orange Juice

1 Margaret Visser, *Much Depends on Dinner* (London, 1989), p. 276.
2 John McPhee, *Oranges* (London, 2000), p. vii.
3 M. Neves et al., IFAMA, *An Overview of the Brazilian Citriculture* (2011), at www.ifama.org, accessed 10 July 2012.
4 Jason Clay, *World Agriculture and the Environment* (Washington, DC, 2004), p. 144.
5 At www.newschief.com, 5 November 2012.
6 'FDA Finds Fungicide in Brazil, Canada Orange Juice', at http://cnn.com, 27 January 2012.
7 Evan D. G. Fraser and Andrew Rimas, *Empires of Food* (New York and London, 2010), p. 162.
8 Visser, *Dinner*, p. 277.
9 Pierre Laszlo, *Citrus* (Chicago, IL, 2007), p. 100.
10 Alissa Hamilton, *Squeezed: What You Don't Know About Orange Juice* (New Haven, CT, 2009), p. 133.
11 Duane D. Stanford, 'PepsiCo Adds Water to Tropicana Products to Juice Margin: Retail' (15 February 2012), at www.bloomberg.com, accessed 10 July 2012.
12 Susan Donaldson James, 'Californian Woman Sues OJ Giant Tropicana Over Flavor Packs' (20 January 2012), at www.abcnews.go.com, accessed 10 July 2012; 'Coca-Cola's "Simply Orange" Faces Lawsuit' (2 April 2012), at www. jdjournal.com, accessed 10 July 2012.
13 Report of 2003, at www.foodcomm.org.uk, accessed 2011.

6 Blossom, Zest and Peel

1 Ann Monsarrat, *And The Bride Wore: The Story of the White Wedding* (London, 1973), p. 115.
2 Ibid., p. 117.
3 Margaret Shaida, *The Legendary Cuisine of Persia* (London, 1994) p. 256.

4 Julia F. Morton, *Fruits of Warm Climates* (Miami, FL, 1987), pp. 130–33.

5 Mary Eales, *Mrs Mary Eales's Receipts* (London, 1773), p. 54.

6 Hannah Glasse and Maria Wilson, *The Complete Confectioner* (London, 1800), p. 345.

7 Tom Jaine, cover illustration for *Petit Propos Culinaires*, 86 (2008).

8 'A New "OPEC" for a Greener Future' (14 September 2011), at york.ac.uk, accessed 9 July 2012.

7 The Poetry of Oranges

1 Samuel Tolkowsky, *Hesperides: A History of the Culture and Use of Citrus Fruits* (London, 1938), p. 10.

2 Ibid.

3 Ibid., p. 116.

4 Ibid., p. 118.

5 In Robert Palter and Jeffrey H. Kaimowitz, trans., *Poemas arabigoandaluces* (Madrid, 1982).

6 Tolkowsky, *Hesperides*, p. 186.

7 In Humbert Wolfe, trans., *Sonnets Pour Hélène* (New York, 1934) p. 69.

8 Mrs Hawkinson, trans., 'Hesperides', *The California Citrograph* (July 1937), cited in Richard H. Barker, 'The First European Book on Citrus', *Citrograph*, 1/4 (July–August 2010), pp. 14–16.

9 Margaret Visser, *The Rituals of Dinner* (London, 1992) p. 287.

10 In Gilbert Sorrentino, *The Orangery* (Austin, TX, 1978).

11 In George Schade, trans., *Fifty Odes* (Austin, TX, 1996).

12 John Dixon Hunt, ed., *The Oxford Book of Garden Verse*, (Oxford, 1993), pp. 237–41.

13 In Alan S. Trebload, trans., *Songs to End With* (New York, 1995).

14 In Wallace Stevens, *Harmonium* (New York, 1923).

15 In W. B. Yeats, *The Wind Among the Reeds* (1899).

16 In George Wallace, *The Milking Jug* (New York, 1989).

17 Ronald Wallace, 'Oranges', *New Yorker* (5 January 1975), p. 70.

18 In *Gastronomica: The Journal of Food and Culture*, 11/4 (November 2002).

8 Art, Design and Culture

1 Tamra Andrews, *Nectar and Ambrosia: An Encyclopedia of Food in World Mythology* (Ontario, 2000), p. 166.

2 Mrs Hawkinson, trans., 'Hesperides', *The California Citrograph* (July 1937), cited in Richard H. Barker, 'The First European Book on Citrus', *Citrograph*, 1/4 (July–August 2010), pp. 14–16.

3 Samuel Tolkowsky, *Hesperides: A History of the Culture and Use of Citrus Fruits* (London, 1938), p. 148.

4 François-René de Chateaubriand, trans. A. S. Kline, *Mémoires d'outre-tombe*, XXXIX/20, at poetryintranslation.com, accessed 10 July 2012.

5 Eliza Haywood, 'Effeminacy in the Army Censured', *The Female Spectator*, 1/2 (1745), p. 104.

6 Tolkowsky, *Hesperides*, p. 282.

7 Ibid., p. 283.

8 John McPhee, *Oranges* (London, 2000), p. 79.

9 Adrian Searle, 'A Momentous, Tremendous Exhibition', *Guardian* (7 May 2002), at www.guardian.co.uk, accessed 10 July 2012.

10 Tolkowsky, *Hesperides*, p. 170.

9 Health and Cookery

1 Mary McCarthy, *Memories of a Catholic Girlhood* (San Diego, CA, 1974), p. 66.

2 'A Boke of Gode Cookery', at www.godecookery.com, accessed 10 July 2012.

3 Samuel Tolkowsky, *Hesperides: A History of the Culture and Use of Citrus Fruits* (London, 1938), p. 160.

4 George Cavendish and Samuel Weller Singer, *The Life of Cardinal Wolsey* (London, 1825), p. 43.

5 George Henry Lewes, *The Life of Maximilien Robespierre* (Chicago, IL and New York, 1849), p. 222.

6 Pierre Laszlo, *Citrus* (Chicago, IL, 2008), p. 87.

7 Theo Clark, chemistry professor at Truman State University, Missouri, reporting to the American Chemical Society (2002), presentation of research paper, *Science Daily*, 3 June 2002.

8 A. R. Proteggente et al., 'The Compositional Characterisation and Antioxidant Activity of Fresh Juices from Sicilian Sweet Orange Varieties', *Free Radical Research*, XXXVII/6 (2003).

9 'The Nutrition Source: Time to Focus on Healthy Drinks', at www.hsph.harvard.edu, accessed 10 July 2012.

10 'Health Tip: Fruit Juices and Kids', www.myfoxdetroit.com, 27 February 2012).

11 Tolkowsky, *Hesperides*, p. 154.

12 Gillian Riley, *A Feast for the Eyes* (London, 1977), p. 45.

13 Tolkowsky, *Hesperides*, pp. 271, 166.

14 Alberto Capatti and Massimo Montanari, *Italian Cuisine: A Cultural History* (New York, 2003), p. 10.

15 Yasmin Doosry, Christiane Lauterbach and Johannes Pommeranz, *Die Frucht der Verheissung*, exh. cat., Germanisches Nationalmuseum, Nuremberg (2011).

16 Tolkowsky, *Hesperides*, p. 272.

17 Capatti and Montanari, *Italian Cuisine*, p. 72.

18 Mark Dawson, *Plenti und Grase* (Totnes, 2009), p. 137.

19 C. Anne Wilson, *Food and Drink in Britain* (Middlesex, 1976), p. 50.

20 Tolkowsky, *Hesperides*, pp. 166–7.

21 Wilson, *Food and Drink*, p. 302.

22 Dawson, *Plenti und Grase*, p. 139.

23 Hilary Spurling, *Elinor Fettiplace's Receipt Book* (London, 2008), p. 69.

24 Barbara Ketcham Wheaton, *Savoring the Past: The French Kitchen and Table from 1300 to 1789* (New York, 1996), p. 30.

25 Ibid., p. 117.

26 Tolkowsky, *Hesperides*, p. 278.

27 Riley, *A Feast for the Eyes*, p. 113.
28 Margaret Visser, *Much Depends on Dinner* (London, 1989),
   p. 267.
29 Helen R. Lane, trans., *Culture and Cuisine* (New York, 1982),
   p. 94.
30 Louis Eustache Ude, *The French Cook* (New York, 1978),
   p. 248.

10 Marmalade

1 C. Anne Wilson, *Food and Drink in Britain* (Middlesex, 1976)
   p. 298.
2 C. Anne Wilson, *The Book of Marmalade* (Totnes, 2010), p. 48.
3 Ibid., pp. 58–61.
4 Ibid., p. 75.

Select Bibliography

Andrews, Alfred C., 'Acclimatization of Citrus Fruits in the Mediterranean Region', *Agricultural History*, xxxv/1 (January 1967)

Laszlo, Pierre, *Citrus* (Chicago, IL, 2007)

McPhee, John, *Oranges* (London, 2000)

Malaguzzi, Silvia, *Food and Feasting in Art* (Los Angeles, CA, 2008)

Riley, Gillian, *A Feast for the Eyes* (London, 1997)

Saunt, James, *Citrus Varieties of the World* (Norwich, 1990)

Stayle, Louise, and Alexis Vaughan, *Taking the Pith* (Sustain Report, 2000)

Susser, Allen, *The Great Citrus Book* (Berkeley, CA, 1997)

Swingle, Walter T., 'The Botany of Citrus and its Wild Relatives', chap. 3 of *The Citrus Industry* (Riverside, CA, 1967), vol. 1

Tolkowsky, Samuel, *Hesperides: A History of the Culture and Use of Citrus Fruits* (London, 1938)

Toussaint-Samat, Maguelonne, *A History of Food* (Chichester, 2009)

Train, John, *The Orange: Golden Joy* (Milan, 2006)

Webber, Herbert John, 'History and Development of the Citrus Industry', chap. 3 of *The Citrus Industry* (Riverside, CA, 1967), vol. 1

Wilson, C. Anne, *The Book of Marmalade* (Totnes, 2010)

Websites and Associations

Citrus Information and Advice

Agrumes Passion (Citrus Passion)
www.agrumes-passion.com

Citrus Categories
www.citrusvariety.ucr.edu/citrus

Citrus Growers Forum
http://citrus.forumup.org

Citrus Identification
http://idtools.org/id/citrus/citrusid

Citrus Pages
http://users.kymp.net/citruspages

Home Citrus Growers
www.homecitrusgrowers.co.uk

Organizations

California Rare Fruit Growers, Inc.
www.crfg.org

Citrus Roots: Preserving Citrus Heritage Foundation
http://citrusroots.com

Florida Oranges
www.floridaorange.com

Museums

Spanish Citrus Historical Museum
www.museonaranja.com

Acknowledgements

I would like to give particular thanks to the following for their help: Susan Haddleton, Richard Laming of the British Soft Drinks Association, the curators at the *Germanisches National-museum,* and 'Millet'.

Photo Acknowledgements

The author and the publishers wish to express their thanks to the below sources of illustrative material and/or permission to reproduce it.

Anaheim Public Library: p. 85; Bibliothèque Nationale de France: p. 31; Bigstock: pp. 6 (taylorjackson), 36 (picturepartners), 38 (dndavis); © The Trustees of the British Museum: p. 16; Coalition of Immokalee Workers: p. 57; Florida Memory: pp. 20, 49, 50, 52, 58, 67, 68, 69, 74, 77, 94, 117; Istockphoto: pp 15 (kizilkaya-photos), 24 (Antonio Jodice), 44 (Daniel Snyder); H. U. Kuenle: p. 18; Library of Congress, Washington, DC: pp. 17, 29, 39, 41, 51, 55, 56; The LuEsther T. Mertz Library at the New York Botanical Garden: p. 28; Orange Public Library: p. 42; Rex Features: p. 61 (Bill Cross/Daily Mail); Victoria & Albert Museum, London: pp. 9, 12, 21, 30, 35, 73, 76, 83, 93.

Index

italic numbers refer to illustrations; **bold** to recipes